Documentum Content Management Foundations

EMC Proven Professional Certification Exam
E20-120 Study Guide

Learn the technical fundamentals of the EMC
Documentum platform while effectively preparing
for the E20-120 exam

Pawan Kumar

BIRMINGHAM - MUMBAI

Documentum Content Management Foundations
EMC Proven Professional Certification Exam E20-120 Study Guide

First published: June 2007

Production Reference: 1310507

Published by Packt Publishing Ltd.
32 Lincoln Road
Olton
Birmingham, B27 6PA, UK.

ISBN 978-1-847192-40-0

www.packtpub.com

Cover Image by www.visionwt.com

Credits

Author

Pawan Kumar

Reviewers

Gaurav Kathuria

Brian Williamson

Senior Acquisition Editor

Douglas Paterson

Development Editor

Nikhil Bangera

Technical Editor

Ved Prakash Jha

Editorial Manager

Dipali Chittar

Project Manager

Patricia Weir

Project Coordinator

Abhijeet Deobhakta

Indexer

Bhushan Pangaonkar

Proofreader

Chris Smith

Production Coordinators

Manjiri Nadkarni

Shantanu Zagade

Cover Designer

Shantanu Zagade

About the Author

Pawan Kumar is a Technical Architect with current expertise in Enterprise Content Management with EMC Documentum. His expertise spans solution architecture, document management, system integration, web content management, business process management, imaging and input management, and custom application development.

Pawan has experience developing products as well as delivering business solutions on the Documentum platform. He is intimately familiar with effective processes and tools for achieving business objectives through Documentum-based technology solutions. He has led and executed requirements and design workshops, architecture design, scoping, estimation, project planning, resource planning, technical design, software development, software testing, solution roll-out, and ongoing support for the deployed solutions. He has also created two products for the Documentum platform.

Pawan has been architecting, designing, and developing enterprise applications for ten years. He has developed software systems for financial services, healthcare, pharmaceutical, logistics, energy services, and retail industries.

Pawan has a BS in Electrical Engineering from the Indian Institute of Technology, New Delhi (India) and MS in Computer Science from the University of North Carolina at Chapel Hill.

Currently, Pawan provides consulting and training services through *doQuent* (http://doquent.com), which was founded with the vision of enabling client success in content-related business initiatives. He also believes in giving back to the community. He founded the free online Documentum community—*dm_cram* (http://dmcram.org), which is a test preparation resource for Documentum exams. He is also an active contributor to the *documentum-users* Yahoo! User group, where Documentum community members seek help for their technical challenges. He can be reached at pk@doquent.com.

Acknowledgement

I dedicate this book to my parents.

This book would not have been possible without the unrelenting support of my wife Rashmi. Working on this book also kept me away from my four-year old daughter Shreya, who often contended with me for using my laptop. My brother Ramesh has been my model of perseverance whenever I needed to keep going in the face of adversity.

I am immensely indebted to the technical reviewers—Gaurav Kathuria and Brian Williamson, for the quality of the contents of this book. Both of them provided painstakingly detailed feedback, which helped improve the accuracy and suitability of the text. Gaurav is the author of *Web Content Management with Documentum*, the book that inspired me to write this one. I have worked with Brian in the past—he is a brilliant Documentum architect and a WDK expert.

The entire Packt team working on this book has made the experience of writing my first book a thoroughly pleasant one. I would like to thank Douglas Paterson, Nikhil Bangera, Abhijeet Deobhakta, Patricia Weir, and everyone else who worked on this book behind the scenes.

I thank Armedia for giving me the opportunity to work with Documentum.

I thank my friends who have been exceptionally patient and understanding while I worked on this book. I particularly thank Sumitra Tyagi, Manmohan Singh, and Katie Leland for their unconditional support and encouragement during some personally and professionally challenging time while I worked on this book.

Finally, I thank the members of dm_cram (`http://dmcram.org`) who confirmed the need for this book.

About the Reviewers

Gaurav Kathuria completed his B. Tech. (Hons.) in Chemical Engineering from I.I.T. Kharagpur in the year 2000 and has since been a prominent performer in diverse software fields, from IT services through product development to software consultancy.

He has a rich experience of designing, developing, and managing software systems using object-oriented languages and technologies like Java/J2EE and Documentum. He started working with Documentum 4i in the year 2001 and has ever since had an extensive experience architecting/designing complex Documentum 4i and 5x projects.

He has also given in-house training on Documentum system architecture, fundamentals, and Web Publisher in many of the organizations he has worked in.

Brian Williamson is a Senior Consultant with Crown Partners. He has extensive experience in both software development and document management. He has worked with Documentum software for a number of years with specialization in both WDK and Web Content Management with Web Publisher. Brian lives in Atlanta with his wife and dogs and in his spare time enjoys reading and baseball.

Table of Contents

Part 1 – Fundamentals

Part 2 – Security

Part 3 – User Interface

Part 4 – Application Development

Part 5 – Advanced Concepts

Practice Tests

Preface

A few years ago (feels like ages now) I dove head first into the EMC Documentum space and was overwhelmed in spite of the significant enterprise technology experience I had under my belt. A simple Documentum deployment involves about five components and there are over 50 products available today in the EMC Documentum suite, not counting the third-party products that have mushroomed around the platform.

I wondered if there was any documentation that would enable me to wrap my arms around this challenge. Indeed, there was documentation—way more than what I was ready to handle as a beginner. I needed something, maybe a book, to get me started in one place and then help me navigate the documentation as a reference by ordering things in an effective fashion.

I am glad to finally see some books on Documentum making it to the market. *Web Content Management with Documentum* by Gaurav Kathuria guides readers in setting up and configuring Documentum for a Web Content Management solution. It also provides an overview of the platform essentials. *A Beginner's Guide to Developing Documentum Desktop Applications* by M. Scott Roth guides readers in desktop application development for Documentum.

When EMC announced the addition of Documentum exams to their Proven Professional certification program, I was excited to see an opportunity to make a contribution. I value certification exams for one benefit above any other—rapid learning. Preparation for these exams exposes the candidate to the breadth and depth of the subject in a short period. Test preparation, when done right, can stimulate rapid growth in knowledge. I consider practice questions and tests to be the best mechanism for identifying gaps in knowledge and, thus, guiding the study effort for maximum effect.

In this book, I share this approach and provide over 250 practice questions to nudge the reader in the directions that would help them the most. I also hope that this book will prove to be a gentle introduction to the breadth of the core Documentum platform and will facilitate entry of technology professionals into the Documentum community.

Pawan Kumar

Introduction

EMC Documentum is the leading **enterprise content management (ECM)** platform globally. EMC Proven Professional certification is an exam-based certification program, which introduced a new EMC Proven Content Management Application Developer (EMCAD) track in early 2007. The first exam in this track is **Content Management Foundations Associate-level Exam**, whose exam code is E20-120.

This book is a complete study guide and includes study material and practice questions to prepare for this exam. Even though this book focuses on certification preparation, it strives to serve Documentum beginners and practitioners irrespective of their interest in the certification exam. It can also serve as a handy guide and quick reference to the technical fundamentals that is fully up to date for Documentum 5.3. Beginners are introduced to concepts in a logical manner while practitioners can use it as a reference to jump to relevant concepts directly.

Enterprise Content Management (ECM)

Content management is a rapidly growing discipline today as new technologies attempt to bring the same rigor to managing *unstructured* content (documents, for example) that databases brought to structured data decades ago. Content management includes various aspects of creating, manipulating, and accessing content including lifecycle and business process automation.

Content lifecycle helps move content through various states, often starting with creation and ending with expiration and archiving. Automating content-centric business processes can bring efficiency to operations and can create a searchable record of events, actions, and performers involved in these processes.

ECM takes these content management aspects to enterprise scales (large number of users, high availability, distributed deployments, high performance, etc.) and enables integration with other systems, which can act as sources or consumers of managed content.

While ECM refers to management of electronic documents in general, several specialized forms of content management have evolved to meet specific needs in more effective ways:

- **Web Content Management (WCM)** is a popular form of content management. It provides rich features for managing web content. For example, web content authors can create content using simple user interfaces without knowing much about technology. The content can be routed to reviewers and approvers and, once approved, can be automatically published to the target website.

- **Record Management** is another form of content management that creates and controls records in various forms that typically serve the legal needs of enterprises.

- **Compliance Management** enables organizations to comply with legal requirements and to prove their compliance with law.

Each of these different forms of content management is implemented on the Documentum platform as a combination of applications and services.

EMC Documentum

Gartner research produces an annual report on the global ECM space. The 2006 report (http://mediaproducts.gartner.com/reprints/emc/vol2/article3/article3.html) forecasts a compound annual growth at 12.8% through 2010 and shows EMC Documentum as the clear leader in this space. EMC has been a well-known leader in enterprise storage hardware and technologies and it has enhanced that position with the acquisition of Documentum. The magic quadrant from the Gartner report is shown in the next figure.

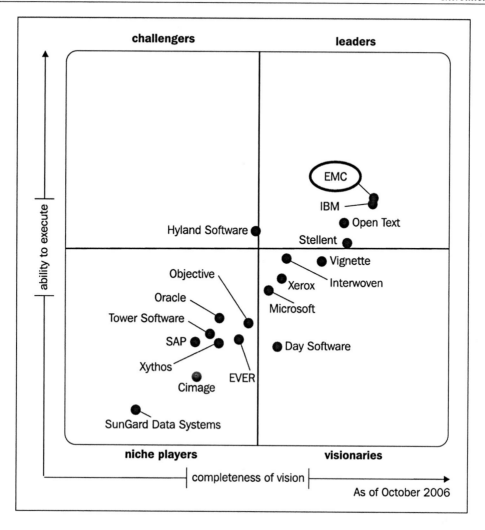

EMC Certification

EMC Proven Professional certification is an exam-based certification program, which has introduced a new **EMC Proven Content Management Application Developer (EMCAD)** track. The first exam in this track is **Content Management Foundations (CMF) Associate-level Exam (E20-120)**. This exam tests knowledge about technical fundamentals of Documentum and is sufficient for achieving the Associate-level certification.

Associate-level certification along with **Content Management Server Programming Exam (E20-405)** grants a Specialist-level certification. Currently only these two exams are available for Documentum. Another exam for Web Development Kit (WDK) programming is expected to become available soon. However, the CMF exam is likely to be a requirement for all Documentum-related certifications.

Why?

What is the value of possessing a certification? Should I take this certification exam? Such questions arise inevitably when one considers working towards any certification.

The answers to these questions are also inevitably specific to the individual asking the question. The answer depends on various factors including the industry, the supply and demand of skilled professionals in the space, the individual's demonstrable experience, and the employer's policies around certifications.

In a rapidly growing niche space like EMC Documentum, demand far outweighs the supply of skilled professionals and this is reflected in the (average) compensation for EMC Documentum services relative to other areas like enterprise Java. As a result, it is a burden on the entity paying for these services to ensure that the services are well worth the costs. A certification provides an assurance of a baseline skill level for the professional providing these services. Therefore, possession of a certification makes the professional's services more marketable.

Along the same lines, a professional seeking to enter the space may have little specific experience to show and may find it hard to compete with people already in this space. Possession of a certification may push the individual's credibility just high enough to provide an opening from where the professional can prove his or her worth.

Irrespective of your reason for taking a certification exam, it would take commitment (and money, currently US$200) to pass such an exam. Certification exams tend to be more academic than reflective of the real-life practice for the subject. Typically, these exams are based on a well-defined syllabus and tend to test the candidate's awareness or understanding of the concepts, though a smaller number of exams are oriented towards the application of the knowledge as well. Real-life practice typically utilizes a small section of the overall subject knowledge (the clichéd 80-20 term comes to mind) and additional knowledge of related areas to make effective use of the subject.

I recall crossing the fence over to the *certified* side with the Java Programmer certification exam about six years ago. The preparation experience was incredibly enriching as well as humbling as I systematically nailed my weak areas and worked on them to come out stronger each time. In the next section, I share this preparation approach that essentially ferrets out and eliminates one's weaknesses.

How?

Now that we know why we should take the certification exam, let's see how to proceed for this exam. You should now be keen to know how to approach and where to register for this professional exam. The following sections will give you the required information.

Approach

Preparation for a professional certification typically competes with other individual responsibilities including work and family. As such, it often becomes an exercise in resource (time, effort, and money) allocation to maximize the results with minimal contention of conflicting demands. In order to make the most of the effort and resources being spent, one needs to prioritize the order in which the topics need attention and the amount of attention required by each topic.

There are probably several good approaches for preparing for exams and their effectiveness varies for individuals due to differences in learning styles. However, I believe that the following approach is a high-level guideline and can be used to tune specific styles of preparation.

If you are familiar with the concept of **bottlenecks** (as in performance tuning) you will easily identify with this preparation approach. Even if this is a new concept for you it is not very difficult to grasp. It is also similar to what is known as **theory of constraints,** where you systematically remove constraints to achieve higher performance relative to the goals. The key concept in the approach is to identify your weakest area (bottleneck or constraint) and spend time and resources on learning about it. Now repeat and move on to the next bottleneck. This won't be an exact science but you should be able to see tangible returns in terms of the new knowledge gained (and improving scores).

As may be obvious to the keen mind, the key step in this process is *identification of the bottleneck.* We need a good tool for identifying our weak areas so that we can focus our efforts and mock tests or practice tests fit this bill wonderfully. Of course, the quality of the questions will matter but if you have a large number of questions to practice with, you are very likely to see the benefits in a short period.

This book attempts to provide a good set of questions to help you focus your learning. Each chapter provides content around the concepts to fill the gaps in your knowledge, but in my opinion the biggest value is added by the rich set of practice questions. Take this approach as a general guideline and tweak your style to make the most out of this book.

Logistics

Once you decide to take this exam, you will need to take care of a few formalities. You will need to register for the exam E20-120 with either of these two:

- *Pearson Vue* (http://www.vue.com)

- *Thomson Prometric* (http://www.prometric.com)

The exam currently costs US$200. Check for your local test center and find the exact details and policies.

Useful Resources

This book offers an economical option that coherently presents the relevant information in one place along with a large number of practice questions. While this book strives to be the key preparation aid for the CMF exam, there are other valuable resources that can help you excel in this exam and carry on the learning process beyond it. Some of these resources are as follows:

1. *dm_cram* (http://dmcram.org) is a free online community to support test preparation for Documentum exams and it offers practice tests, useful tips, and discussion forums.

2. *Product documentation* is a good reference whenever you need to learn about a concept or clarify a doubt. It may be hard to read the documentation end to end like a book. The following product documents may be worthwhile to reference in your preparation—Content Server Fundamentals, Content Server Administration Guide, Content Server Object Reference, Content Server DQL Reference, Documentum Application Builder User Guide, User Guide/Help for Webtop and Documentum Administrator, Documentum System Development Guide, and Documentum Architecture White Paper.

    However, the number of documents and their level of detail have made it challenging to use them efficiently and effectively as a study aid.

3. *EMC Documentum training*—Technical Fundamentals of Documentum (`http://mylearn.documentum.com/portals/home/ml.cfm?actionID=38&courseID=23844`) is the course recommended by EMC for preparing for this exam. EMC Documentum training is a great resource as well, though it is a relatively expensive option.

4. *documentum-users* (`http://groups.yahoo.com/group/documentum-users/`) is a very active user group (Yahoo! Groups) where the Documentum community members ask questions and share their knowledge and expertise.

5. *dm_developer* (`http://dmdeveloper.com/`) is another online community where members ask questions and share their knowledge and expertise. It also features technical articles and case studies.

What This Book Covers

This book is organized in chapters based on the structure of the recommended training for the CMF exam (`http://mylearn.documentum.com/portals/home/ml.cfm?actionID=65&subjectID=3259`).

The chapters are grouped together in parts to provide a logical grouping and order of topics as described below.

Part 1: Fundamentals (Chapters 1 - 4)

ECM Basics introduces the basic concepts of content management. *Working with Content* describes the aspects of creating and manipulating content. *Objects and Types* lays the foundation of designing and using metadata. *Architecture* describes the key components of the EMC Documentum platform and how they interact to provide the content management capabilities.

Part 2: Security (Chapters 5 - 7)

Users and Privileges describes the core concepts related to users for implementing security in Documentum. *Groups and Roles* provides additional capabilities for facilitating security management for groups of users. *Object Security* introduces permissions and ties them to users, groups, and privileges to realize the security model.

Part 3: User Interface (Chapter 8)

Searching describes the features for finding relevant content stored in a repository. While other user interface aspects are covered throughout the book, searching is described separately because of its fundamental importance to content management.

Part 4: Application Development (Chapters 9 - 12)

Custom Types describes how to create user-defined metadata structures and fundamental customization aspects. *DocApps* describes how to package the development artefacts for reuse and portability across repositories. *Workflows* and *Lifecycles* describe how to model and implement business processes in Documentum.

Part 5: Advanced Concepts (Chapters 13 - 14)

Aliases describes a mechanism for dynamic assignment of ownership, locations, and permissions. *Virtual Documents* describes how multiple documents can be managed as one larger document to facilitate collaboration.

There are two practice tests at the end of this book.

There is a set of questions at the end of each chapter. These questions are meant to test your understanding. A good way to prioritize and focus your efforts is to use the questions to identify the areas where you score low and then work on those areas.

The answers to all the questions and the solutions to the practice tests have been provided at the end.

Conventions

In this book, you will find a number of styles of text that distinguish between different kinds of information. Here are some examples of these styles, and an explanation of their meaning.

There are three styles for code. Code words in text are shown as follows: "Each Content Server client that installs the DFC runtime has a local file named `dmcl.ini`."

A block of code will be set as follows:

```
SELECT user_name, user_login_name, user_state
FROM dm_user
WHERE user_login_name = 'jdoe'
```

New terms and **important words** are introduced in a bold-type font. Words that you see on the screen, in menus or dialog boxes for example, appear in our text like this: "In this example, John gets permissions in four ways—as the owner of the object, as a specific user, as a member of a specific group, and as an implicit member of **World**."

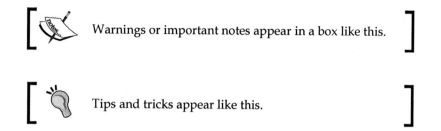

Warnings or important notes appear in a box like this.

Tips and tricks appear like this.

Reader Feedback

Feedback from our readers is always welcome. Let us know what you think about this book, what you liked or may have disliked. Reader feedback is important for us to develop titles that you really get the most out of.

To send us general feedback, simply drop an email to feedback@packtpub.com, making sure to mention the book title in the subject of your message.

If there is a book that you need and would like to see us publish, please send us a note in the **SUGGEST A TITLE** form on www.packtpub.com or email suggest@packtpub.com.

If there is a topic that you have expertise in and you are interested in either writing or contributing to a book, see our author guide on www.packtpub.com/authors.

Customer Support

Now that you are the proud owner of a Packt book, we have a number of things to help you to get the most from your purchase.

Errata

Although we have taken every care to ensure the accuracy of our contents, mistakes do happen. If you find a mistake in one of our books—maybe a mistake in text or code—we would be grateful if you would report this to us. By doing this you can save other readers from frustration, and help to improve subsequent versions of this book. If you find any errata, report them by visiting http://www.packtpub.com/support, selecting your book, clicking on the **Submit Errata** link, and entering the details of your errata. Once your errata are verified, your submission will be accepted and the errata added to the list of existing errata. The existing errata can be viewed by selecting your title from http://www.packtpub.com/support.

Questions

You can contact us at questions@packtpub.com if you are having a problem with some aspect of the book, and we will do our best to address it.

Good luck! Let's get started.

Part 1

Fundamentals

ECM Basics

Working with Content

Objects and Types

Architecture

1
ECM Basics

In this chapter, we will explore the following concepts:

- Content and metadata
- Repository and Content Server
- Various features of the Documentum platform

This chapter introduces key content management concepts in Documentum terminology. The concepts are described at a high level to provide an overview of the breadth of the platform. These concepts are explored in detail in the following chapters.

Content and Metadata

Databases are ubiquitous in modern technology solutions. This is a mature field and well-known best practices are routinely used for deploying databases. Databases provide standard means for accessing and manipulating structured data. *Structured* means that the data components (fields) are of specific type (integer, string, etc.) and this knowledge helps in querying and manipulating the data.

On the other hand, files stored on the file system are generally *unstructured* and can contain information in any form. Such files and the unstructured information contained therein are collectively referred to as **content**.

While databases provide standard means of managing structured data, **content management systems (CMS)** are a relatively new phenomenon. Since the content itself is unstructured, it is not possible to read and understand the content without any prior knowledge about it. Therefore, some structured data is attached to each content item, which describes the content item. This data that provides information about the attached content item is called **metadata**.

Content management systems utilize metadata extensively to provide sophisticated functionality. For example, metadata is essential for making documents searchable in terms of their author, title, subject, or keywords. It is hard to imagine any functionality of Documentum that does not utilize metadata in one form or another. The following figure shows two content items and their associated metadata:

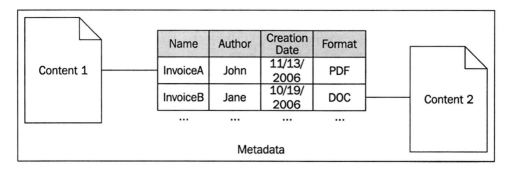

Name	Author	Creation Date	Format
InvoiceA	John	11/13/2006	PDF
InvoiceB	Jane	10/19/2006	DOC
...	...	...	...

Metadata

Repository

Content management systems need to manage both content and metadata. EMC Documentum uses the host file system (by default) to store the content and a database to manage metadata and its association with the content items. Note that the content can also be stored in other types of storage systems, including a Relational Dababase Management System (RDBMS), a content-addressed storage (CAS), or external storage devices.

EMC coined the term *content-addressed storage* (CAS) in 2002 when it released its Centera product. CAS provides a digital fingerprint for a stored content item. The fingerprint (also known as an ID or logical address) ensures that it is exactly the same item that was saved. No duplicates are ever stored in CAS.

A **repository** is a managed unit of content and metadata storage and includes areas on the file system and a database. However, the details of the organization of the files and metadata in a repository are hidden from the users and applications that need to interact with the repository. The repository is managed and made available to the users and applications via standard interfaces by a Content Server process. The following figure shows the basic structure of a repository:

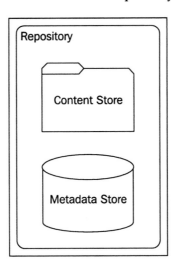

The repository was known as **docbase** in pre-5.3 versions of the Documentum platform. These two terms are used interchangeably by the Documentum community.

Content Server

Content Server serves content to applications, which in turn provide friendly interfaces to human users. Content Server brings the stored content and metadata to life and manages its lifecycle. It exposes a known interface for using the content while hiding the details of how and where files and metadata are stored.

The term *Content Server* is used in two contexts — the Content Server *software* that is installed and resides on the file system and the Content Server *instance*, which is the running process that resides in memory and serves content at run time. However, there is little chance of confusion since the usage is often clear from the context and the term *Content Server* is typically used without additional qualification (software or process/instance).

A Content Server instance is dedicated to and manages only one repository. However, we will see later in architecture discussion that multiple Content Server instances can be dedicated to the same repository. This is typically done for performance reasons where the multiple Content Server processes divide up the load for serving content from the same repository. The following figure shows two Content Servers serving one repository:

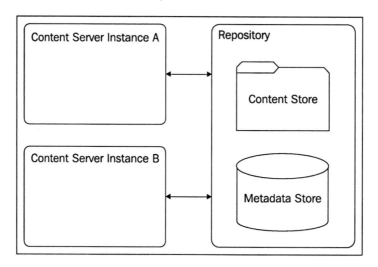

Content Server is the foundation of the Documentum platform and provides the following services:

1. Content management services
2. Process management services (workflows)
3. Security service for content and metadata in the repository
4. Distributed services

These features are described here briefly and in more detail in later chapters.

Content Management Services

Content management services include library services (checkin and checkout of objects stored in the repository), version control, and archiving. The Content Server uses an object-oriented model and stores everything as an object in the repository.

Metadata can be retrieved using **Document Query Language (DQL)**, which is a superset of Structured Query Language used with databases (ANSI SQL). DQL can query objects and their relationships, in addition to any database tables registered to be queried using DQL.

Data dictionary stores information about object types in the repository. The default data dictionary can be altered by addition of user-defined object types and properties. *Properties* are also known as *attributes* and the two terms are used interchangeably to refer to metadata.

Virtual documents link multiple component documents together into a larger document. An individual document can be part of multiple virtual documents. The assembly of virtual documents can also be controlled by business rules and data stored in the repository.

Collaborative services can be deployed with an optional license and make collaboration features available in client applications. Collaborative features (Documentum 5.3) include:

- *Room*: This is a secured area within a repository with defined membership and access restrictions.

- *Discussion*: This is a comment thread associated with an object.

- *Contextual folder*: This is a folder with attached description and discussion.

- *Note*: This is simple document with built-in discussion and rich text content.

 Documentum 6 is expected to introduce new collaborative features such as polls and calendars.

Retention Policy Services (RPS) is an optional product and enables use of policies to manage the lifecycle of the objects stored in the repository. A retention policy defines the phases through which such an object passes and how it is finally disposed of or exported.

Process Management Services

Process management services (features) include the following:

- **Workflows**: Workflows typically represent business processes and model event-oriented applications. Workflows can be defined for documents, folders (representing the contained documents), and virtual documents. A workflow *definition* acts like a *template* and multiple workflow *instances* can be created from one workflow definition.

- **Lifecycle**: A lifecycle defines the stages through which a document passes. For each stage, *prerequisites* can be defined and *actions* can be defined that are performed prior to an object's entry into that stage.

Security Services

A repository uses **access control lists (ACLs),** also known as **permission sets,** as the security mechanism by default. The repository security can be turned off as well.

While the repository security model is ACL, each object has an associated ACL. The ACL provides object-level permissions to users and groups.

When the repository security is enabled, the Content Server enforces seven levels of *basic permissions* and six levels of *extended permissions.* There are additional *privileges* and security components, which are discussed in later chapters.

Content Server provides robust accountability and capability via auditing and tracing facilities. **Auditing** can track operations such as checkin or checkout that have been configured to be audited. **Tracing** can provide detailed run-time information useful for debugging applications.

Electronic signatures can enforce *sign-offs* in business processes. A sign-off is a way of authorizing or approving a decision similar to signing off on paper.

Distributed Services

A Documentum *installation* can include multiple repositories and the Content Server is aware of distributed configurations that deployments can take.

The Content Server provides an **application programming interface (API)** and therefore needs a layer in front of it to expose its capabilities to human users. Documentum provides *desktop* and *web-based* client applications and supports creation of custom applications of either type. The following figure shows several client applications:

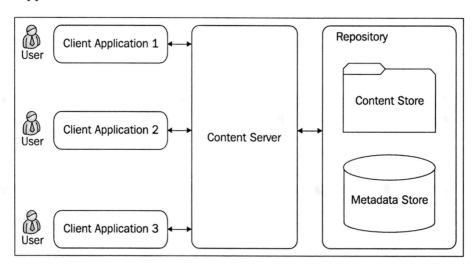

The full set of Content Server features is exposed via **Documentum Foundation Classes (DFC)** and **Documentum Client Library (DMCL)**. DFC provides the API for interacting with the Content Server programmatically.

Documentum also provides a Web Development Kit (WDK) to facilitate development and customization of web-based client applications.

Documentum provides two interactive utilities for interacting with the Content Server using queries—**IDQL** and **IAPI**. These utilities are typically used by administrators and developers.

Checkpoint

At this point you should be able to answer the following key questions:

1. What is content and what is metadata?
2. What is a repository and what is Content Server? What is the relationship between the two?
3. What services are provided by EMC Documentum platform? What features are enabled by these services?

Test Your Understanding

1. A comma-separated value (CSV) file is not content since it contains structured information (True/False).
2. Where is metadata stored in a repository?
    a. Files
    b. File properties
    c. Database
    d. None of the above
3. Content and metadata are served by the repository (True/False).
4. Which of the following statements are correct?
    a. One Content Server instance can serve two repositories
    b. One repository can be served by two Content Server instances
    c. One Content Server instance can serve only one repository
5. DQL can be used to query database tables (True/False).

6. The collaborative service feature(s) offered by the Content Server is/are:
    a. Discussions
    b. Calendars
    c. Chat
    d. Notes

7. Workflows can be defined for:
    a. Documents
    b. Jobs
    c. Folders
    d. Lifecycles

8. Content Server provides accountability features via:
    a. Jobs
    b. Audit trail
    c. Tracing
    d. Documentum Administrator

9. Documentum offers the following interactive query utilities:
    a. WDK
    b. IDQL
    c. DMCL
    d. IAPI

10. The default repository security mechanism is:
    a. ACL
    b. Permission set
    c. Alias set
    d. Login

2
Working with Content

In this chapter, we will explore the following concepts:

- Importing and exporting content
- Checking out and checking in
- Versioning
- Formats and renditions

We have placed this chapter before *Objects and Types* (Chapter 3) because it is more intuitive to think about working with files than with the metadata associated with them. However, there are some concepts in this chapter that refer to object properties. We recommend that you revisit these concepts after going through *Objects and Types* (Chapter 3).

Interacting with Content

Content and metadata stored in the repository are managed and served by the Content Server. However, human users interact with the Content Server through several types of applications. Depending upon their roles, the users may use one of the following means to interact with the Content Server:

1. A web application such as Webtop or Documentum Administrator. This is the most common means of interacting with the Content Server.
2. A desktop application such as Documentum Desktop.
3. A query tool such as IDQL or IAPI. These tools are often used by administrators or developers for precise and low-level interaction with the Content Server.

4. A custom application, which uses DFC or integration technologies (EMC Documentum Business Process Services, EMC Documentum Web Services Framework, etc.) to interact with the Content Server. Such an application may provide higher-level operations appropriate for the business, which bundle multiple low-level operations in some sequence.

Irrespective of the interface used by the end users, the Content Server offers the same core capabilities to all entities directly interacting with it. This is shown in the following figure:

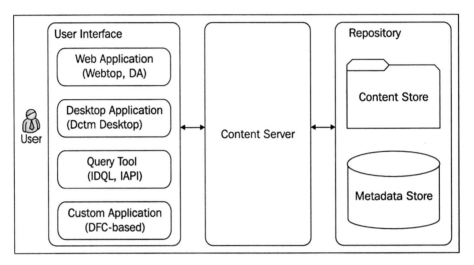

These core capabilities are the subject of this chapter, though their typical manifestation via Webtop is also described.

Importing Content

Importing content into a repository brings it under the management of the Content Server. This is how content existing outside the repository gets added to the repository.

Importing results in a new Documentum object containing metadata for this content item and the content item is associated with this object. This object gets version labels 1.0 and CURRENT. Versions are described later in this chapter.

Exporting Content

Exporting content from a repository creates a copy of the content outside the repository, typically on a file system. This is how content is copied outside the repository and this external copy is no longer associated with the content inside the repository. This operation does not modify the content inside the repository.

Checking Out

Checking out a content item from the repository allows it to be modified by the user performing the checkout. This operation **locks** the content item in the repository (in an exclusive manner), preventing other users from modifying the content item. The user checking out the item is known as the **lock owner** for that item.

Applications such as Webtop also create a copy of the content outside the repository, typically on a user's desktop where the user can work on this content item. Other users can still access the locked object or any of its versions for viewing or exporting.

Conventionally, applications display a checked-out item with a *key* for its lock owner. Other users see a *lock* on the item. This is shown in the following figure:

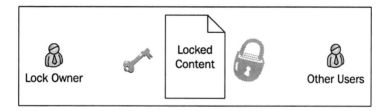

Typically, the application checking out the item for a user remembers the association of the external copy with the Documentum object that was checked out. The primary purpose of checking out content is to modify the content and then check it back in as an update. A user working on modifying the content can take a long time before the content is ready to be checked back into the repository. Therefore, the application needs to utilize this *memory* at the time of checking in to identify the object being updated.

 Applications like Webtop also have an **edit** operation, which checks out the document and launches an appropriate application, based on the format of the document, to edit the document. In this process, Content Server is only involved in the checkout step.

A checkout can also be canceled. **Canceling checkout** results in the lock being released from the document and no changes are made to the document in the repository. All changes made locally may be discarded. A checkout can be canceled by the **lock owner** or a **superuser**. We will learn about superusers in the chapters dealing with security.

Checking In

An item checked out for modification can be checked into the repository. This operation applies the changes to the content stored in the repository.

Content Server maintains a history of the changes applied to objects using **versions**. When a checked out object is checked back in, a new version is created. Each version is a separate object (content and metadata) but is aware of the object from which it was created. A **version tree** is a visualization of multiple versions derived directly or indirectly from the same root object. *Duplicate versions* are not allowed in a version tree, since the purpose of the version tree is to enable distinction among objects based on their versions. Versioning is described in detail in the following section.

Applications such as Webtop offer several options for altering the behavior of checkin:

1. The user can choose not to create a new version and replace the existing content with the content being checked in.
2. The user can choose to increment the major version or the minor version. See the next section for information about major and minor versions.
3. The user can choose to make the new version the current version for the version tree.
4. The user can choose to keep the object checked out for more changes (also known as *retain lock* as opposed to *release lock*).
5. The user can add another version label.
6. The user can modify the metadata for the new version.

The following additional options are also available:

1. The user can keep a local copy of the document.
2. The user can subscribe to the document. *Subscriptions* provide bookmark-like functionality and are described in *Searching*.
3. The user can manually select another local file to use as the new content.

[Checkout and checkin are also referred to as **library services**.]

Versioning

As mentioned earlier, importing or creating a new object creates the version 1.0 for that object. This object becomes the root of the version tree that will be created by checking out and checking in this object and the versions derived from this object. Each version is a separate object with its own content and metadata. The versions are as shown:

1.0 ⟶	1.1 ⟶	1.2 ⟶	2.0

The Content Server applies an **implicit version label** to each object in the repository and the label is of the form *Major.minor*. Additional **symbolic version label**s can be added to an object's metadata, which are descriptive and more appropriate for the end user.

If the checkin operation increments the *minor* version, the *major* portion is left unchanged. For example, the version label changes from 2.3 to 2.4 when the object is checked in as minor version. If the checkin operation increments the major version, the minor portion is reset to 0. For example, the version label changes from 2.3 to 3.0. In general, the version labels of the form x.0 are referred to as **major versions** and the others are referred to as **minor versions**.

Normally, checkin sets the new version as the **current version**. However, an older version can be left as current instead. Typically, applications and DFC queries use the current version as the default where multiple versions could be considered. Applications require explicit actions for accessing non-current versions.

[A folder object inside the repository cannot be versioned. However, applications can allow users to *check out a folder* with the semantics that the documents linked to that folder need to be checked out. This is just a usability enhancement for the user interface.]

Branching

Branching enables users to work from an older version while still retaining the latest changes. However, as we will see in a moment, branching is a part of the version numbering scheme rather than a feature for end users.

Content Server allows checking out a version older than the highest one. When this object is checked in, two options are available as usual — check in as major version or as a minor version. If major version is chosen, the next higher (higher than the highest major version present) major version is used. If minor version is chosen, there are two possibilities — the next minor version is already present or it is not.

If the next minor version is not present, that one is just used. However, if the next minor version is already present, a **branch** is created in the version tree. The sequence of versions *splits off* as a new branch at this point. The version for the checked in object at the point of branch origin is obtained by appending .1.0 to the implicit version of the object that was checked out.

Let's look at an example to clarify these concepts. For the version tree shown in the next figure, assume that the versions were created in this order — 1.0, 1.1, 1.2, 2.0, 1.1.1.0, 1.1.1.1. Now consider the point in time just after 2.0 was created. The version 1.1 was checked out and then checked back in as a minor version. The next minor version, 1.2, was already present in the version tree, so a branch was created with version 1.1.1.0. Note that even though this label ends in .0 it is a minor version.

Major versions have this form — x.0. If a major version were selected for checkin, no branch would be created and the new version would be 3.0. Further, if 1.2 were checked out and then checked in as minor (1.3) or major (3.0) version, no branch would be created. Checking in a branch also defaults the new version to CURRENT.

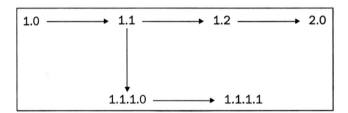

 If a second branch is created at the same branch point as the first one, the new version will be created by appending 2.0, and so on.

Once there are branches in the version tree, checking in becomes more interesting. Incrementing minor version works in the same way, with the rightmost number getting incremented. However, incrementing the major version results in the next higher major version after the highest major version in the complete tree. So 2.3.1.6 can lead to 5.0 if 3.0 and 4.0 are already present in the version tree. This is obvious once we remember that duplicate version numbers are not allowed in a version tree.

 When a branch is being created, it is not possible to check in the document as the same version.

How can we find out if two objects are part of the same version tree? In other words, how can we know whether two objects represent different versions of the same root object? Each object has a unique identifier called object ID stored in a property (metadata element) called r_object_id. Each object in a version tree has a property called i_chronicle_id. All the objects in a version tree have the same value of this property and it is the value of the r_object_id property of the root object in the version tree. These two properties are demonstrated in the following figure:

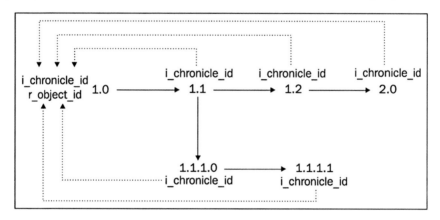

Another property important for versioning is i_antecedent_id, which relates a version to its previous version (*parent*) in the tree. We will learn more about objects, properties, and object relationships in later chapters.

Formats

A **format** identifies the organization of document contents. Typically, it is used to identify the application that can understand the contents of the document and use it meaningfully. Within Documentum, a format captures information such as file name extensions related to the format. For example, *pdf* and *doc* are document formats.

Renditions

Each content item has a **primary format**. However, it is possible to represent the same document in other formats and attach it to the same object. These other formats (non-primary formats) are called **renditions**. Thus, it is possible to have *text* and *pdf* renditions of a document whose primary format is *doc*.

> Differences between the renditions are not limited to format, though it is probably the most common criterion; other criteria can be resolution (for images) and language (for translations).

Renditions can neither be *edited* nor *versioned*.

A rendition is not stored as a separate object within the repository. Each rendition is attached to one object representing the primary format. In fact, the only properties tied to a rendition are the object ID of the primary format and the format of the rendition itself. This is shown in the following figure:

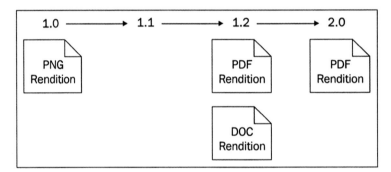

Rendition generation can be automated by installing additional EMC Documentum software components:

- DTS: Document Transformation Services can create PDF and HTML renditions.
- ADTS: Advanced DTS adds more formats to the list supported by DTS.
- MTS: Media Transformation Services can create various media formats, such as a TIFF file from a Photoshop file.
- Custom converters: Custom converters can be plugged in to support formats not covered by the above services or to use alternative means of creating these renditions.

Documentum Product Notes

Content Server offers the content-related operations in fine granularity. Most of the options described above for these features (such as options available on checkin) are offered by applications such as Webtop, which bundle these together as one unit.

Similar considerations apply to portions of the interaction that take place on the user's desktop. For example, launching an application to view or edit content is a capability of the client application and not of the Content Server.

DTS, ADTS, and MTS are optional EMC Documentum products for converting one format into another and for creating renditions.

Checkpoint

At this point you should be able to answer the following key questions:

1. What are the core Content Server features for working with content?

2. What is the difference between import and checkin? What is the difference between export and checkout?

3. What are versions? What is a version tree? What are branches?

4. What are formats? What are renditions?

Test Your Understanding

1. When a new content item is imported it gets the following version label automatically:

    a. 0.1

    b. 1.0

    c. NEW

    d. CURRENT

2. The following operations create a copy of the content item outside the repository:

    a. Import

    b. Export

    c. Checkout

    d. Cancel Checkout

3. There can only be one lock owner for one object (True/False).

4. Only the lock owner can cancel a checkout (True/False).

5. A checkin always results in a new version of the document (True/False).

6. If the following versions are all present in a version tree, which of these can be the CURRENT version:

    a. 1.0

    b. 1.1

    c. 2.0.1.0

    d. 2.1

7. What can be the new version if a folder at version 1.3 is checked in:

    a. 1.4

    b. 2.3

    c. 2.0

    d. None of the above

8. If version 3.4 of an object is checked out, it can be checked in with the following new version:

    a. 3.5

    b. 4.0

    c. 5.0

    d. 3.4.2.0

9. Which of the following aspects of a document identifies the editing application for the document:

    a. Version

    b. Format

    c. Rendition

    d. Object type

10. The i_chronicle_id property of a rendition identifies:

    a. r_object_id of the root object of the version tree

    b. r_object_id of the previous version

    c. version label of the previous version

    d. None of the above

3
Objects and Types

In this chapter, we will explore the following concepts:

- Objects and types
- Type hierarchies
- Object persistence
- Querying objects

Objects

Documentum uses an object-oriented model to store information within the repository. Everything stored in the repository participates in this object model in some way. For example, a user, a document, and a folder are all represented as objects. An **object** stores data in its **properties** and has **methods** that can be used to interact with the object.

A content item stored in the repository has an associated object to store its metadata. For example, a document stored in the repository may have its title, subject, and keywords stored in the associated object. However, note that objects can exist in the repository without an associated content item. Such objects are sometimes referred to as *contentless objects*. For example, a user object or a permission set object does not have any associated content.

Note that the term *method* may be used in two different contexts within Documentum. A method as a defined operation on a type is usually invoked programmatically through DFC. There is also the concept of a method representing code that can be invoked via a job, workflow activity, or a lifecycle operation. This qualification will be made explicit when the context is not clear.

Each object property has a data type, which can be boolean, integer, string, double, time, or ID. A boolean value is true or false. A string value consists of text. A double value is a floating point number. A time value represents a timestamp, including dates. An ID value represents an object ID that uniquely identifies an object in the repository.

A property can be **single-valued** or **repeating**. Each single-valued property holds one value. For example, the object_name property of a document contains one value and it is of type string. This means that the document can only have one name. On the other hand, keywords is a repeating property and can have multiple string values. In this example, a document can have object_name='invoice.pdf' and keywords='invoice.pdf','ABC Corp.','Trading'.

The following figure shows a visual representation of this object. Typically, only properties are shown on the object while methods are shown when needed.

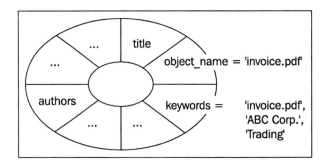

r_object_id is a special property of every persistent object. It is used to uniquely identify an object and encodes some information within the property itself. It is a 16-character string value where each character is a hex (hexadecimal) digit. The first two digits constitute a *tag* representing the *type* of the object.

For example, 09 means that the object has a type that is dm_document or its subtype—the object represents a document rather than a user, group, or something else. Subtypes are explained later in this chapter. The next 6 digits represent the *repository ID*—a numeric identifier assigned to the repository. The last 8 digits represent a *unique ID within the repository* and this ID is generated by the Content Server.

Note that EMC Documentum assigns a unique range of repository IDs to each of its customers for the various repositories served by their Content Server installations. As long as these assigned repository IDs are used uniquely, r_object_id will uniquely identify an object across all repositories.

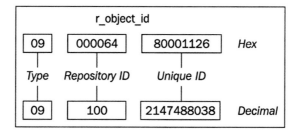

Methods are operations that can be performed on an object. An operation often alters some properties of the object. For example, the checkout method can be used to check out an object. Checking out an object sets the r_lock_owner property with the name of the user performing the checkout. Methods are usually invoked using Documentum Foundation Classes (DFCs) programmatically, though they can be indirectly invoked using DQL and API.

Object Types

Different objects may represent different kind of entities — one object may represent a workflow while another object may represent a document, for example. As a result, these objects may have different properties and methods. Each time an object is created in the repository, it needs to be determined what properties and methods it is going to have. This information comes from an **object type**.

An object type is a template for creating objects. In other words, an object is an *instance* of its type. A Documentum repository contains many predefined types and allows addition of new user-defined types (also known as *custom* types). User-defined types offer important capabilities and are described in detail in a separate chapter — *Custom Types*.

The most commonly used predefined object type for storing documents in the repository is dm_document. Objects in a repository can be organized using **folders**, which are stored as objects of type dm_folder. The root folder in a folder tree is called a **cabinet** and is stored as an object of type dm_cabinet. Users are represented as objects of type dm_user in the repository. A group of users is represented as an object of dm_group. Workflows use a process definition object of type dm_process, while the definition of a lifecycle is stored in an object of type dm_policy. These object types are described in more detail at various places in later chapters.

Here is a figure displaying the object types:

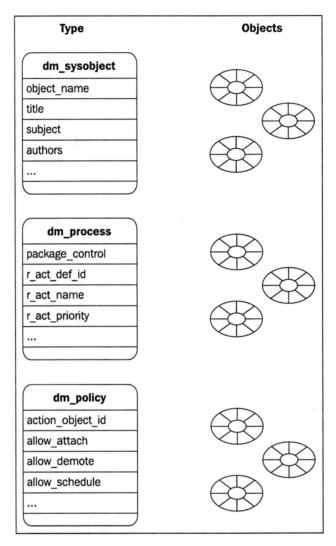

While the obvious use of a type is to define the structure and behavior of one kind of objects, there is another very important application of types. A type can be used to refer to all the objects of that type as a *set*. For example, queries restrict the scope of search by specifying a type and as a result only the objects of that type are considered for the results. Queries are introduced later in this chapter.

As another example, audit events can be restricted to a particular object type resulting in only the objects of this type being audited. Auditing is described in more detail in *User and Privileges* (Chapter 5).

Type Names and Property Names

Each object type uses an *internal type name*, such as dm_document, which is used for uniquely identifying the type within queries and application code. Each type also has a *label*, which is a user-friendly name often used by applications for displaying information to the end users. For example, the type dm_document has the label Document. Conventionally, internal names of predefined (defined by Documentum) types start with dm_.

Just like an object type each property also has an internal name and a label. For example, the label for property object_name is Name. There are some additional conventions for internal names for properties. These names may begin with the following prefixes:

1. r_: (read only) This prefix normally indicates that the property is controlled by the Content Server and cannot be modified by users or applications. For example, r_object_id represents the unique ID for the object. On the other hand, r_version_label is an interesting property. It is a repeating property and has at least one value supplied by the Content Server, while others may be supplied by users or applications.

2. i_: (internal) This prefix is similar to r_ except that this property is used internally by the Content Server and normally not seen by users and applications. As discussed in the last chapter, i_chronicle_id binds all the versions in a version tree together and is managed by the Content Server.

3. a_: (application) This prefix indicates that this property is intended to be used by applications and can be modified by applications and users. For example, the format of a document is stored in a_content_type. This property helps Webtop launch an appropriate desktop application to open a document. The other three prefixes can also be considered to imply *system* or non-application attributes, in general.

4. _: (computed) this prefix indicates that this property is not stored in the repository and is computed by Content Server as needed. These properties are also normally read-only for applications. For example, each object has a property called _changed, which indicates whether it has been changed since it was last saved. Many of the computed properties are related to security and most are used for caching information in user sessions.

Type Hierarchy

It is common for different types to be related in some sense and share properties and methods. In true object-oriented style, Documentum allows persistent types to be organized in an **inheritance**-based **type hierarchy**. A type can have one **supertype** and inherit all the supertype properties as its own. The complete set of properties belonging to a type is the union of the inherited properties and properties explicitly defined for that type. In this relationship, the new type is called a **subtype**.

The *super* and *sub* prefixes are based on the visual representation of this relationship where the supertype is positioned logically higher than the subtype, as shown in the following figure:

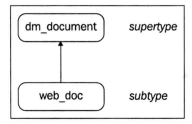

Note that supertype and subtype are *relative* terms. This means that when using either of these terms we refer to two types. A type can be a *subtype* for one type and *supertype* for another type at the same time. When many of these related relationships are visually represented together, they create a structure similar to an inverted tree (root at the top) known as a *type hierarchy*. Readers familiar with object-oriented modeling will recognize this type hierarchy as a *class-inheritance hierarchy*. The following figure shows a portion of the type hierarchy for the predefined Documentum types:

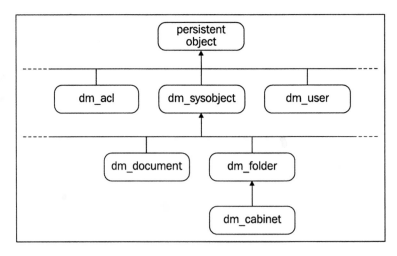

`dm_document` is an important type since it is almost always involved with document storage and that is a key capability of the Documentum platform. It is an interesting type because it has no properties of its own and it inherits all its properties from `dm_sysobject`.

One may question the point of having a separate type without any properties of its own. Remember the comment about using a type for treating the objects of that type as a set? `dm_document` as a separate type enables us to refer to all the objects of this type and subtypes as a set. It can also be used for the complementary set, for example, identifying all the objects of type `dm_sysobject` but not of the type `dm_document`.

Object Persistence

Objects that are stored in the repository are called **persistent** objects and their types are referred to as persistent types. All persistent types are part of a type hierarchy rooted in the internal type *persistent object*, which has the following properties:

1. `r_object_id`: This is used for unique identification, assigned to the object by the Content Server. This property is described earlier in this chapter.

2. `i_vstamp`: This is used internally for version control; it holds the number of committed transactions that have altered this object.

3. `i_is_replica`: This is used in replication and determines whether an object is a **replica** of another in a different repository. Object **replication** replicates (copies) objects, both content and metadata, from a source repository to a target repository. The object copies in the target repository are known as replica objects.

Objects are stored in the repository using **object-relational technology** where properties are stored in (relational) database tables. Each persistent type is represented by two tables in the repository database — one for storing the single-valued properties and the other for storing the repeating properties. Single-valued properties for a type are stored in a table named *type_name*_s, while repeating properties are stored in a table named *type_name*_r.

For both single-valued and repeating properties, the property names map to the column names in the tables. Further, all of the _s and _r tables also have a column named `r_object_id`. The `r_object_id` column is used to join the single-valued and repeating properties along with the inherited properties to bring all the properties of an object together.

The structure of the _r tables is worth paying extra attention to. Each object can have multiple rows in the _r table where each column represents one repeating property. Usually, two repeating properties of an object are not related to each other. For example, authors and i_folder_id are two repeating properties of dm_sysobject and there is no relation between an author and the ID of a folder that the object is linked to. Yet, these two values may be present in the same record in dm_sysobject_r.

This storage scheme of shared records lets us determine the number of records for an object in its _r table. It is equal to the maximum number of values in any of the repeating properties that is not an inherited property for the object's type.

The following figure illustrates persistence for an object of a custom type my_course:

my_course_s

course_id	credits	r_object_id
CS100	3	0900006480001126

my_course_r

r_object_id	instructor_id	location_id	prereq_id
0900006480001126	CSI121	LT112	MA100
0900006480001126	CSI102	LT134	
0900006480001126	CSI092		

Note that the tables used for persisting objects of a particular type only store the properties explicitly defined for that type. Inherited properties are stored in the tables for the supertypes where they belong. Since dm_document does not have any properties of its own, there is no table named dm_document_s or dm_document_r in the repository database.

It is useful to know how properties are stored in database tables but all the properties of objects can be queried together using DQL without any reference to these tables. Internally, the Content Server uses database views that join appropriate tables to retrieve all the needed properties of the type together.

While most of the types represent persistent objects, there are some types whose objects are used for temporarily storing information in memory. These objects are not stored in the repository and are called **non-persistent** objects. For example, collection objects are used to store query results and they reside only in memory at run time.

Querying Objects

Document Query Language (DQL) is a query language for Documentum just as Structured Query Language (SQL) is a query language for databases. In fact, DQL is a superset of ANSI SQL, which means that a valid query in ANSI SQL is also a valid DQL query. DQL queries can be executed using IDQL (Interactive DQL shell), Documentum Administrator, Webtop, or programmatically through DFC applications.

DFC provides a rich set of functionality for interacting with objects, including creating, querying, and modifying objects. DFC is a programmatic means of interacting with objects and is used in applications. DQL is used both for scripting and with DFC in applications. In this section, we will examine some DQL queries used for manipulating objects. However, this is just a small overview of DQL capabilities and the *DQL Reference Documentation* should be used to explore the full set of DQL capabilities.

SELECT Query

A DQL query can be used to inspect or affect one or more objects in a repository. The most common type of DQL query is the SELECT query, which retrieves the properties of one or more objects. For example, consider the following query:

```
SELECT r_object_id, r_creation_date
FROM dm_document
WHERE object_name = 'mydoc.txt'
```

This query shows three keywords — SELECT, FROM, and WHERE. These keywords divide up the query into three parts:

1. *SELECT clause (selected values list)*: The selected values list specifies the properties to be retrieved.
2. *FROM clause*: The FROM clause specifies the object types to be queried.
3. *WHERE clause*: The WHERE clause is optional and specifies the conditions for the objects to meet whose properties will be returned by the query. When the WHERE clause is present, the query is also called a *conditional* query.

A DQL query can also directly query database tables, though the tables need to be registered first. A **registered table** is a table from the underlying database that has been registered with the repository. This registration allows the table to be specified in a DQL query, either by itself or in conjunction with a type. A registered table can be used as an object type and its columns can be used as properties.

Now, let's try to understand the semantics of this query. The FROM clause specifies that we want to consider objects of type dm_document. Among these objects, we only want to look at objects that have 'mydoc.txt' in their object_name property. The query will return the object ID (r_object_id property) and creation date (r_creation_date property) for all the resulting objects.

No matter how (DFC or DQL) objects are queried, Content Server always enforces the configured security. Content Server will not return all documents just because a query requests all documents. It will only return the documents that the currently authenticated user is allowed to retrieve.

The same rules apply to the operations other than querying. Repository security is discussed in more detail in later chapters.

Basics

The comma-separated list after SELECT identifies the values to be returned. These values typically come from object properties, though they may include constants and calculations on properties as well. The allowed properties depend on the types specified in the FROM clause. For example:

```
SELECT object_name, title
FROM dm_document
```

Here the selected values are the properties object_name and title for the type dm_document. It is possible to rename the values being returned using the following syntax:

```
SELECT object_name AS Name, title AS Title
FROM dm_document
```

This capability is more useful and desirable when multiple types are present in the FROM clause:

```
SELECT d.r_object_id AS ObjectId, f.r_object_id AS FolderId
FROM dm_document d, dm_folder f
WHERE ...
```

Note that the selected values are both r_object_id, so renaming enables us to distinguish between them. Also note that we need to associate the property name with the type name in this case and it is done by using the prefixes d. and f., where d and f are *aliases* (unrelated to the aliases in alias sets to be discussed in later chapters) for the types in the FROM clause. It is a good practice to use aliases for types and prefix them to property names when multiple types are present in the FROM clause.

It is rare to run a select query without a WHERE clause because it will return all objects of the specified type(s). The WHERE clause enables us to provide conditions or search criteria and narrow down the search scope to find the specific objects we are looking for.

WHERE Clause

The WHERE clause specifies a condition, which may consist of multiple conditions that an object must satisfy to be a part of the result set. An object participates in the conditions via its properties. Functions, expressions, logical operations, and literals are used along with the properties to define the condition. Some examples below illustrate the usage of WHERE clause.

The following example shows the use of a string literal in the WHERE clause. Note that a string literal is placed within single quotes:

```
SELECT object_name
FROM dm_document
WHERE title = 'CS100'
```

The following example shows that a numeric value does not use quotes. This query retrieves objects that have been updated at least once:

```
SELECT object_name
FROM dm_document
WHERE i_vstamp > 0
```

An object ID literal is placed within single-quotes. The following query retrieves one specific object from the repository using its object ID:

```
SELECT object_name
FROM dm_document
WHERE r_object_id = '0900006480001126'
```

A repeating property in a WHERE clause is typically used with the keyword ANY, as shown in the next example. This query retrieves all documents that have any of the keywords set to invoice:

```
SELECT object_name
FROM dm_document
WHERE ANY keywords = 'invoice'
```

Another commonly used condition relates to dates and the DATE function is useful for such situations. The following query retrieves objects that have not been modified since 12/10/2006:

```
SELECT object_name
FROM dm_document
WHERE r_modify_date < DATE('12/10/2006')
```

Next we look at UPDATE queries, which are used for modifying objects.

UPDATE Query

An UPDATE query updates one or more objects and has the following syntax:

```
UPDATE <type_name> OBJECT
<property_updates>
WHERE <condition>
```

The WHERE clause works just as in the SELECT query. As before, the WHERE clause is optional but it is highly recommended that the WHERE clause should not be omitted as far as possible. <type_name> is the type or an *ancestor type* (supertype or supertype's supertype, and so on) of the object(s) to be updated. <property_updates> specify the property names and the corresponding values to be set. The following example illustrates these concepts:

```
UPDATE dm_document OBJECT
SET object_name = 'mydoc.txt',
SET title = 'John''s Document',
SET authors[0] = 'John',
SET authors[1] = 'Jane'
WHERE r_object_id = '0900006480001126'
```

This query shows several new features. Note that the keyword OBJECT (OBJECTS is also acceptable) is required, since we are trying to update the objects. If OBJECT is omitted, the query will attempt to modify the type (rather than objects). <property_updates> is specified using the format SET <property_name> = <value>. If multiple properties are being updated they are separated using commas.

Another point to note is that if a repeating property, like authors in this example, needs to be updated, each individual value needs to be set using this format— SET <property_name>[<index>] = <value>. <index> specifies the position in the list of repeating values for the property and the positions start with 0. Also note that for title we used two apostrophes where we needed one in the value. It is true for all DQL queries that an apostrophe inside a string literal should be replaced with two to escape the special meaning of the apostrophe.

It is not common to distinguish between a supertype and an ancestor type. Often, the term supertype is intended to mean "supertype, supertype's supertype, and so on". The term subtype is also loosely used in a similar fashion to include the descendants in the type hierarchy.

DELETE Query

A DELETE query is similar to an UPDATE query except that there are no properties to be set. A DELETE query has the following format:

```
DELETE <type_name> OBJECT
WHERE <condition>
```

This query does not have many new features. In fact it is probably one of the simplest DQL queries. Again, the WHERE clause is optional but omitting it will result in all objects of the specified type and its subtypes being deleted. You need to be very careful when using DELETE queries. Let's look at an example of the DELETE query:

```
DELETE dm_document OBJECT
WHERE owner_name = USER
AND FOLDER('/Temp')
```

This query deletes all objects of type dm_document or any of its subtypes that are owned by the currently authenticated user and linked to the folder path /Temp. Note the use of the keyword USER—it gets dynamically replaced with the currently authenticated user when the query is executed. Similarly, TODAY is a keyword that gets replaced with the date on which the query is executed. Some other useful keywords are YESTERDAY, TOMORROW, and NOW. These keywords are used in queries that utilize date or time values.

Further, note the use of keyword AND—it enables conjunction of two conditions in the WHERE clause. OR and NOT can also be used in a similar manner.

A **path** within a repository is represented in a way similar to a path on the file system. For example, /Temp/mydocs/resume.doc is a path in the repository to a document named resume.doc. This document is *linked* to a folder named mydoc, which in turn is linked to a cabinet named Temp.

The top-level folders are special and are called cabinets. They always appear as the first element in a path. Each repository has some cabinets created for use by Documentum software. These cabinets are called *system* cabinets. Temp is a system cabinet, which is frequently used for organizing temporary objects.

The query also illustrates how to search certain folders for objects. The folder predicate can specify one or more folder paths and whether the subfolders of those folders should be included in the search recursively. Consider the modified version of this query:

```
DELETE dm_document OBJECT
WHERE owner_name = USER
AND FOLDER('/Temp/a','/Temp/b',DESCEND)
```

This query deletes all objects of type dm_document or any of its subtypes that are owned by the currently authenticated user and linked to the folder path /Temp/a or /Temp/b or any subfolders of these paths. Note that multiple folders can be specified in the folder predicate and, optionally, DESCEND specifies that the subfolders should be included.

API

API methods can be issued via IAPI or Documentum Administrator in addition to programmatic access through DFC. IAPI can send individual method calls to the server. The API can be used to create scripts for administrative or development purposes. One of the most common uses of the API is to dump an object to view all of its properties. For example, the following API command prints the names and values for all the properties of the object identified by the given object ID:

```
dump,c,'0900006480001126'
```

The API will not be discussed in detail in this book. For exploring the API in detail, please see the *API Reference Documentation*.

Documentum Product Notes

DQL queries can be executed through IDQL, Documentum Administrator, or Webtop. They can also be executed programmatically using DFC.

API queries can be executed using IAPI, Documentum Administrator, and DFC.

Checkpoint

At this point you should be able to answer the following key questions:

1. What is the difference between objects and types? How are objects related to types?

2. What information is encoded in the r_object_id attribute?

3. What is a type hierarchy? How are objects persisted in the repository database?

4. What are the various ways of querying the objects in a repository? What are some common DQL queries?

Test Your Understanding

1. An object can inherit properties and methods from another object (True/False).

2. There is no dm_folder_s table (True/False).

3. Administrators can use DQL to query the objects that DFC would prevent them from accessing due to permission restrictions (True/False).

4. Suppose a custom type my_document is a subtype of dm_document. When an object of type my_document is created, the first two hex digits of r_object_id for this object will be _____.

5. The prefix i_ for predefined properties normally indicates:

    a. Immutable
    b. Internal
    c. Imported
    d. None of the above

6. Suppose a document has only three of its repeating properties set:

    ```
    authors='John','Jane';
    keywords='invoice','corporate','finance','software';
    r_version_label='1.2'.
    ```

    Given that all of these properties are present in dm_sysobject_r, how many records will this object have in this table?

    a. 1
    b. 2
    c. 4
    d. 8

7. The dm_document_r table stores the authors property since authors is a repeating property (True/False).

8. The first two hex digits in `r_object_id` represent:

    a. Repository ID

    b. Unique ID within the repository

    c. Object format

    d. None of the above

9. DQL can be used to query databases directly (True/False).

10. The following query will include a `dm_document` object named `mydoc.txt` in the result set as long as its permissions allow it (True/False):

    ```
    SELECT r_object_id, title
    FROM dm_sysobject
    WHERE object_name = 'mydoc.txt'
    ```

4
Architecture

In this chapter, we will explore the following concepts:

- Documentum architecture layers
- Platform components
- Communication patterns

Documentum Platform

The term *Documentum* means different things to different people. Some people think of the repository, some think of Webtop, and the others think of a custom content application they are exposed to.

In order to grasp the full capabilities and organization of Documentum, it is best to think of it as a set of *core product components*, an additional set of *optional product components* (some of which are frequently used), and an unbounded set of *custom applications*.

EMC offers over 50 product components for the Documentum platform. In order to make this complexity manageable, from the standpoint both of comprehension and of software maintenance, the platform is also organized as a framework. The framework provides guidelines, standards, and tools for using and extending the platform.

The Documentum platform is organized in layers, just like the well-known *n-tier* architecture for enterprise applications. The similarity is more in terms of the benefits of using layers and less in terms of the traditional tiers. As we will see, some Documentum layers span multiple tiers.

Layered Architecture

Layered architectures are a norm in enterprise applications today. Layers can separate components by various criteria such as purpose or role, technology, and dependence on other components. There are various benefits of layered architectures including:

- Complexity becomes manageable from multiple perspectives—comprehension, design, implementation, testing, and deployment.

- Encapsulated implementation of a layer makes it possible to replace the layer with another implementation.

- Multiple higher-level layers can utilize the functionality of the lower-level layers, thus promoting reuse.

In this discussion, we will use the term *tiers* in the popular sense—*presentation* (*view*), *logic*, and *persistence* (*data/content storage*). We will describe the Documentum platform architecture in terms of layers.

The Documentum platform is organized in four layers—**Repository Layer, Content Services Layer, Component and Development Layer,** and **Application Layer.** Each layer serves a specific purpose and consists of product components that contribute towards that purpose. The following schematic figure illustrates Documentum architecture organized in layers, which are explored in more detail in the rest of this chapter:

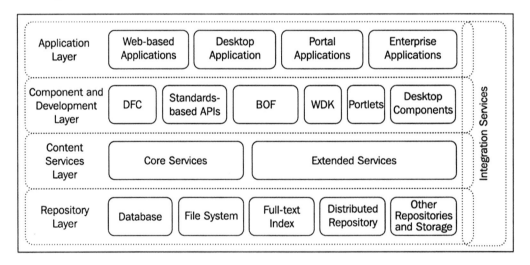

The following figure maps Documentum architecture layers to traditional architecture tiers. Note how some layers span multiple tiers.

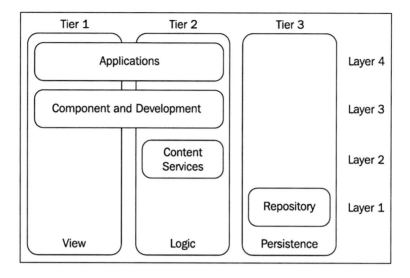

Repository Layer

The **Repository Layer** provides storage for the platform and consists of the *content repository*, which uses **file stores** and a relational database as its components. The file store is a logical storage area and can be a file system of the host operating system (OS) or a **Content-Addressed Storage (CAS)**, such as EMC Centera. CAS uniquely identifies a content item using a digital fingerprint (also known as ID or logical address) of the content item rather than a file system path of the content item. Other alternatives such as streaming servers and even relational databases can be used as file stores.

Optionally, the repository can also maintain a **full-text index** of all text-based content assets stored within the repository. For example, such content may include documents, text files, HTML files, XML content, and close-captioned video content.

In a Documentum deployment, the Content Server, the file store, and the database can all be hosted on separate physical machines. All normal access to the repository should occur through the Content Server. In order to avoid accidental or malicious direct access, the content storage on the file system is secured by permissions to the **installation owner** only. The installation owner is the OS user account used for installing Content Server.

Content Services Layer

As discussed in a previous chapter, a repository is brought to life by the *Content Server*. The Content Server manages the repository and provides a low-level interface for interaction with the repository. The **Content Services Layer** (also referred to as **Services Layer**) provides application-level services for organizing, controlling, sequencing, and delivering content to and from the repository.

The Content Services Layer consists of the following core services:

- **Library Services**: These services consist of checkin/checkout, versioning, and basic rendering. These concepts are discussed in *Working with Content* (Chapter 2).

- **Security Services**: These services consist of authentication, authorization, and auditing. These concepts are discussed in the chapter related to security.

- **Workflow Services**: These services automate business activities and policies for repository content. Workflows are discussed in Chapter 11.

- **Lifecycle Services**: These services automate the lifecycle policies of the repository content. They assign a lifecycle state to a content item and then manage its transitions from one state to another according to the lifecycle policy. Lifecycles are discussed in Chapter 12.

- **XML Services**: These services provide essential features for managing XML content items in their native format and include:

  - **XML content validation**: XML validation ensures that XML elements are well-formed and conform to the associated definition (i.e. DTD or Schema).

  - **XML chunking**: Chunking segments XML documents into their elements, which are then managed as discrete content objects.

Additionally, the content services layer includes the following extended services:

- **Repository Services**: These services include the following:

  - **Retention Policy Services (RPS)**: RPS uses policies to automate retention and disposal of content objects.

  - **Trusted Content Services (TCS)**: TCS enables handling of application-specific security requirements through file store encryption, digital shredding, electronic signatures, and extension of the underlying security model.

- **Enterprise Content Integration (ECI)** services for federated search: These services consist of a framework of adapters for various internal and external repositories and enable searching multiple heterogeneous repositories together. These repositories include non-Documentum repositories such as FileNet or LexisNexis repositories.

- **Content Transformation Services (CTS)**: These services convert various kinds of content from one format and resolution into others. For example, these content types may include documents, images, and videos. CTS consist of several modules, including these most common ones:

    - **Document Transformation Services (DTS)**: DTS supports document transformations such as Microsoft Office documents to PDF and HTML.

    - **Advanced Document Transformation Services (ADTS)**: ADTS extends DTS by adding support for additional formats—Microsoft Project, Microsoft Visio, AutoCAD, and multi-page TIFF.

    - **Media Transformation Services (MTS)**: MTS provides rich media transformations and analysis for static digital assets, including photos, scanned images, and Microsoft PowerPoint slide decks.

- **Content Intelligence Services (CIS)**: These services analyze the text within documents and other content objects and automatically set their metadata. They can also categorize these documents according to predefined rules.

- **Site Delivery Services**: These services deliver and deploy content to web servers, portals, and application servers. These services include:

    - **Site Caching Services (SCS)**: SCS enables delivering content to disparate delivering environments.

    - **Site Deployment Services (SDS)**: SDS complements SCS by automatically delivering content to multiple external web servers or web server farms.

- **Collaboration Services**: These services enable multiple users to work on common documents in the repository together. These services use specialized collaborative objects, which include rooms, discussion threads, contextual folders, and notes.

Component and Development Layer

The **Component and Development Layer**, also known as **Interface Layer**, provides access to the repository content and the content services. This layer consists of predefined components and their application programming interfaces for enabling customization, integration, and application development. This layer consists of Documentum Foundation Classes (DFC), a set of standards-based APIs, Business Object Framework, WDK, Portlets, and Desktop components.

Documentum Foundation Classes

Documentum Foundation Classes (DFC) expose the Documentum object model as an object-oriented library for applications to use in the form of Java and Component Object Model (COM) libraries. DFC provides higher-level capabilities such as *virtual document management*, *XML content-management*, and *business objects*. Virtual documents combine component documents into a larger document. Virtual document management is described in the chapter *Virtual Documents* (Chapter 14).

Standards-Based APIs

This layer also provides standards-based APIs, which include the following:

- **Java Database Connectivity (JDBC)**, **Open Database Connectivity (ODBC)**, and **ActiveX Data Objects (ADO.NET)**: These APIs make a repository appear as a database and make it accessible in the form of a relational database.

- **Web-based Distributed Authoring and Versioning (WebDAV)**: WebDAV is an extension of the HTTP protocol that enables web-based distributed access to content. The Documentum platform includes a WebDAV server, which provides access to a repository via the WebDAV protocol.

- **File Transfer Protocol (FTP)**: Documentum includes an FTP server that enables content exchange with the repository using the FTP protocol.

- **File Share Services**: These services make a Documentum repository look like a network drive, enabling simpler access to the repository via desktop applications.

- **Web Services Framework**: This framework provides application developers with an environment for developing content-related components and for making them available using web-based standards such as WSDL, SOAP, and XML.

  ° **Web Services Description Language (WSDL)** is a standard for describing a web service in XML, which is used by client applications to utilize the web service.

  ° **Simple Object Access Protocol (SOAP)** is a standard for exchanging XML-based messages over computer networks, usually using HTTP.

The web services components enable other systems to interact with Documentum over the Web. A web service is easily accessible to client applications running on diverse platforms. For example, a client application running on .NET can easily interact with a web service without the need for a .NET to Java Bridge.

Business Object Framework

Business Object Framework (BOF) is a structured environment for developing content applications. BOF enables developers to create reusable components that can be shared by multiple applications.

Documentum supports two types of business objects:

1. **Type-based Business Object (TBO)**: TBOs are the most common types of business objects. They are tightly linked to an existing or custom object type. New methods (custom business logic) can be added to such a type via a TBO. For example, business objects representing a customer, partner, or an agreement are all suitable to be implemented as TBOs.

2. **Service-based Business Object (SBO)**: An SBO implements logic of procedures that are not specific to an object type. In fact, an SBO typically interacts with objects of multiple types in order to accomplish its function. Another way to think about SBOs is that they provide global or common services to multiple object types in a repository.

   For example, the Documentum Inbox service is an SBO and is not tied to a particular type of object. Any SBO can easily be made available as a web service as well.

Other Components

The Component and Development Layer includes WDK, desktop components, and portlets in addition to the components we have already discussed. Let's have a look:

- **Web Development Kit (WDK)** is a library of components as well as a framework for developing J2EE web applications on the Documentum platform. The WDK components provide basic web application functionality for interacting with content and allow custom applications to be built on top of it. The custom applications are able to add to and alter the behavior provided by WDK.

  The Documentum web application products such as Webtop, Documentum Administrator (DA), Web Publisher (WP), Digital Asset Manager (DAM), Records Manager, Documentum Compliance Manager (DCM), etc. are also built on the WDK framework.

- **Desktop components** provide a base library and framework for developing desktop applications for Documentum.

- **Portlets** are pluggable user interface components that are managed and displayed in a web portal. Portlets enable Documentum applications to be presented within a portal user interface.

Application Layer

The Component and Development Layer builds the bridge to the content services layer for applications that are part of the Application Layer. It is the **Application Layer** that makes the platform available to human users. The application layer essentially opens up the platform for any type of use that can utilize content-management capabilities. The Applications in this Layer can be categorized into web-based applications, desktop applications, portal applications, and enterprise applications.

Some such existing applications are described in the next section, while more custom applications can be created using the capabilities made available by the Component and Development Layer.

Webtop is the essential web application for interacting with a repository. Webtop is a WDK application and is built on top of the WDK components. Documentum Administrator is very similar to Webtop but provides additional administrative capabilities for managing repositories.

Digital Asset Manager (DAM) is another WDK application with specific capabilities for managing digital media such as presentations, brochures, marketing communications, etc. Web Publisher (WP) is a WDK application for managing web content with Documentum. It provides a model and framework for managing content with appropriate user roles and an interface that can hide technical details from content creators, reviewers, and approvers. Records Manager is a WDK application with specific focus on content that needs to be managed as records.

Documentum eRoom is a web-based collaboration application, which can operate independently of the Documentum platform. However, it can also utilize the platform for underlying document-management capabilities. Each eRoom in the application provides a collaborative workspace for a team, where tools such as document sharing, common calendars, polls, and discussion threads are available. The default Documentum eRoom interface is available through a web browser and an optional client plugin enhances its user interface.

Documentum Desktop is the basic desktop interface to the repository and it is built on top of the desktop components in the Component and Development Layer.

Integration Services

Documentum offers options in all layers for integration with other systems providing the flexibility and granularity needed to meet business and technical requirements. Integration Services span the four layers and do not constitute a separate layer. The layers are as follows:

1. The Application Layer has access to the full range of capabilities offered by the Component and Development Layer. There are several dedicated Documentum integrations available for popular enterprise applications such as SAP and Siebel. Custom integrations can also be developed using WDK or DFC components.

   For example, a loan management financial application can utilize the document management capabilities of the Documentum platform. A custom integration can create an interface suitable for the financial application and utilize DFC to interact with the repository. Once this integration is in place, the financial application can create, update, retrieve, and delete documents with appropriate metadata within a Documentum repository.

2. The Component and Development Layer provides integration options via FTP, WebDAV, JDBC, ODBC, ADO.NET, and the Web Services Framework. These options provide different ways to make content services and repository available to other systems via standards-based APIs.

3. The Content Services Layer provides the following services:

   ° File Share Services: File Share Services make a repository available as a file share.

   ° Business Process Services (BPS): BPS facilitates integration with Workflows and offers enhanced features such as integration with JMS, SMTP, etc.

   ° Directory Integration Services: Directory Integration Services facilitate integration with user directories for utilizing common infrastructure for implementing security within Documentum.

4. The Repository Layer provides integration options through **Content Storage Services**. These services open up the options available for implementing varied storage features for persisting and sharing content and metadata. Content Storage Services add a storage policy engine to the repository to automate storage allocation and migration based on policies.

   For example, frequently accessed content can be stored in a high-performance storage environment while rarely accessed content can be migrated to a more economical storage environment.

Communication Patterns

Operation of the Documentum platform involves basic communication patterns, which are repeated over and over. In order to understand these patterns, it is important to first identify the components that participate in such communication.

Key Components

The following figure shows the key components involved in communication with Content Server:

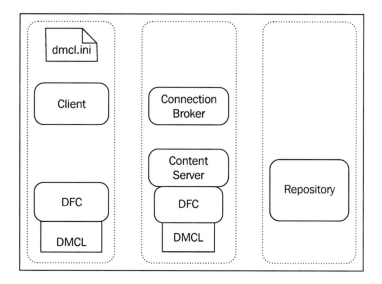

We are already familiar with the Content Server—it manages the repository. Any content management communication ultimately needs to reach it.

Documentum Client Library (DMCL) is a low-level API that exposes full Content Server functionality. DMCL supports Remote Procedure Call (RPC) capability, enabling clients to connect to the Content Server without dealing with network details. Even though direct access to DMCL is available, it is not recommended for clients to directly interact with DMCL. Rather DFC wraps around DMCL and exposes a higher-level API for the clients to use.

DFC is implemented in Java and it also provides a *Java-COM Bridge* for access from Visual Basic or Visual C++. It also provides a **Primary Interop Assembly (PIA)** that supports access from the .NET platform. Every Documentum client uses an instance of DFC running locally within a Java Virtual Machine (JVM). DFC also has server-side logic, hence runs a copy on the Content Server as well.

A client is any application or component that connects to the Content Server.

A **Connection Broker** (formerly known as **DocBroker**) is Documentum's *name server* or *registry* and it provides information and status of Content Servers to clients. When a Content Server is started, it announces its status to the connection broker(s) it is configured to *project* to. The connection broker records this status of the Content Server.

Each Content Server client that installs the DFC runtime has a local file named dmcl.ini. This file contains the name and port of a connection broker. Optionally, it can contain information about additional (also known as secondary) connection brokers.

Fundamental Communication Pattern

The fundamental communication pattern with a Content Server is illustrated in the following figure, where the arrows indicate the flow of data:

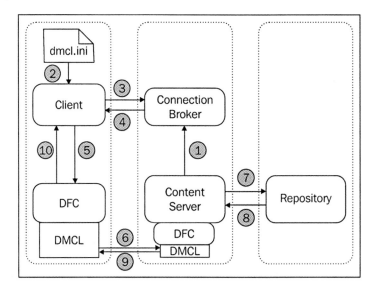

The different stages in the flow of data are as follows:

1. The first piece of communication takes place when a Content Server starts up. It informs the configured connection brokers about its status. This communication from a Content Server to a connection broker is called **projection**. This communication is initiated by the Content Server and does not involve a client.

2. When a client needs to connect to this Content Server, it reads dmcl.ini for the name and port of a connection broker. The client can contact multiple connection brokers.

3. The client requests the connection broker to give information about the Content Server.

4. The connection broker sends information about the Content Server instances.

Note that this interaction is not explicit in the sense that the client doesn't have to perform each of these steps individually and explicitly. Actually, these steps are typically performed by DFC functionality while the client just invokes the appropriate higher-level interface for this purpose.

5. The client now sends this information to the Documentum Foundation Class (DFC), which has Documentum Client Library (DMCL) linked to it. DMCL can perform network communication using the RPC capability.

6. This client-side DFC communicates with the DFC on the Content Server side. A request is sent to the Content Server via DMCL.

7. Once the Content Server receives the request made by the client, it processes it and interacts with the repository by sending a request. This request may involve interaction with the database and the file stores that constitute the repository.

8. The repository responds to the request by providing the required information to the Content Server.

9. The DFC on the Content Server side passes this information to the client-side DFC. This communication takes place with the help of DMCL.

10. Once the processing is completed, client-side DFC returns the results to the client.

The client can continue to interact with the same Content Server, without returning to the connection broker again.

Once the session ends or a new Content Server needs to be contacted, the pattern starts from the beginning.

WDK Application Communication Pattern

WDK is a library and framework for developing J2EE web applications for Documentum. A WDK application runs in a J2EE-compliant application server (more specifically, a *servlet engine*). A WDK application is organized into components where each component consists of the following:

1. Component XML configuration
2. Pages that are part of the component presentation
3. Java classes encoding the behavior of the component
4. Resource bundles for localization

A WDK application is also organized in layers and each layer has a directory (folder) of its own on the file system. The foundation layers of WDK applications are wdk and webcomponent on top of that.

For example, Webtop has the following layers (in order):

1. wdk: The wdk layer provides the base WDK framework layer.

2. webcomponent: The webcomponent layer provides components for the core web interface.

3. webtop: The webtop layer provides interface and behavior specific to the Webtop application.

4. custom: The WDK framework is designed to be extended and customized and the custom layer is provided specifically for this purpose.

    A separate layer for customization prevents upgrades from overwriting the custom code. It also keeps most of the customization code together under one folder. The customization model supports small and selective customization, as well as large scale behavior and user interface changes.

A user usually interacts with a WDK application through a browser. In this case, the browser is not a client of the Content Server, since it is communicating with the application server. It is the WDK components on the application server that are the clients for the Content Server. The communication between the WDK components and the Content Server follows the same fundamental pattern. Indeed, there is dmcl.ini on the application server while there need not be any on the computer running the browser.

In summary, the browser client may interact with the WDK application in any pattern but the WDK components interact with the Content Server in the same fundamental pattern as described earlier.

Documentum Product Notes

The interaction of Content Server with a repository deserves some attention. One Content Server serves one repository but multiple Content Server instances can also serve the same repository. This is usually done for performance reasons (*load balancing*) where the expected number of concurrent requests to one instance may cause it to become overloaded.

Multiple Content Server instances may also be used for high availability (*failover*) where failure of one Content Server instance doesn't make the repository unavailable since the other instance(s) can serve the repository.

The Content Server is supported by **Method Servers,** which can execute **methods.** In this context, a method is a piece of code that can be scheduled to run as a job or can be invoked from a workflow activity or a lifecycle action. Let's see the following Method Servers:

- **Dmbasic Method Server**: This executes methods written in **Docbasic.** Docbasic is a programming language, somewhat similar to Visual Basic, supported by Documentum. A Docbasic program can access the Content Server functionality via API calls.

- **Java Method Server**: This executes methods written in Java. However, these methods are not literally the methods on a Java class. A Documentum Java Method is a class that implements a specific interface in order to be accepted as a Documentum Java Method. The Java Method Server is just a J2EE application server (currently Apache Tomcat) that hosts the web applications responsible for executing Documentum Java methods.

The Content Server is supported by an optional **Index Server** that can perform **full-text indexing** on the content stored in the repository. Full-text indexing a document means that the contents of the document are analyzed and the results of the analysis are stored as indexes. The full-text indexes make it possible to search for documents based on the contents of the documents. The Index Server also indexes metadata attributes.

Index Agents coordinate the interaction between Content Server and Index Server.

By default, the Documentum platform embeds the FAST Index Server as the Index Server. However, the search capability is modular and alternative choices are possible. For example, an open-source search engine, Lucene, is used in the new Documentum Content Server OEM edition that can be embedded by other vendors in their applications.

Checkpoint

At this point you should be able to answer the following key questions:

1. What are the four layers of Documentum architecture? What are their roles? What are the key components of each layer?

2. What is the fundamental communication pattern for interacting with the Content Server? How is it different from interaction with a WDK application?

Test Your Understanding

1. The layers of Documentum architecture map one-to-one on the tiers of application architecture (True/False).

2. The following layers are part of the Documentum platform layers:

   a. Application layer

   b. Connection layer

   c. Content Services layer

   d. Repository layer

3. The following product provides the ability to search for words inside document contents:

   a. Java Method Server

   b. Content Server

   c. Index Server

   d. Content Intelligence Services

4. BOF is a part of DMCL (True/False).

5. DFC is written in Java but it can be accessed from the .NET platform using:

   a. Java-COM Bridge

   b. Primary Interop Assembly

   c. Connection Broker

   d. DMCL

6. Which of the following is true:

   a. Content Server projects to connection broker

   b. Connection broker projects to repository

   c. Repository projects to Content Server

   d. Repository projects to connection broker

7. A client finds out about available connection brokers using:

   a. `server.ini`

   b. `client.ini`

   c. `dmcl.ini`

   d. `dmconnbroker.ini`

8. The following component performs the network communication when communicating with the Content Server:

    a. DFC

    b. BOF

    c. DMCL

    d. WDK

9. When using a WDK application, the Content Server client is:

    a. Browser

    b. WDK component

    c. JSP

    d. Servlet

10. The default name of the customization layer in WDK applications is:

    a. `wdk`

    b. `customwdk`

    c. `customcomponent`

    d. `custom`

Part 2

Security

Users and Privileges

Groups and Roles

Object Security

5

Users and Privileges

In this chapter, we will explore the following concepts:

- A high-level view of Documentum security
- Users and authentication
- User authorization including privileges and client capabilities
- User management

Documentum Security

At a high level, the security model in Documentum is similar to that used in contemporary enterprise applications. There are *resources* (information, objects) that need to be secured, there are *operations* that can be performed on the resources, and there are *users* who wish to perform these operations. The *security configuration* defines what is allowed for various combinations of users, operations, and resources. At run time, a user attempts to perform an operation and the components of the Documentum architecture resolve rules for the specific user, operation, and resource combination to allow or disallow the attempted operation.

At a detailed level, security implementation is very specific to the Documentum architecture. This is the first chapter on Documentum security and introduces the concept of users and security aspects that are tied to users.

Security, in general, involves two parts—**authentication** and **authorization**. While authorization deals with what a user is allowed to do, the first step is to identify the user reliably. Therefore, first the user *identity* is authenticated and then each attempted operation by this user is checked against the authorization rules configured for this user.

Just like everything else, security configuration is also stored in the repository as objects and properties on objects. Various components of the Documentum architecture enforce the configured security rules. In some cases, it may be possible to use external (non-Documentum) components to assist with security enforcement. For example, an LDAP server or a product such as eTrust SiteMinder can participate in the user authentication process. This is an important feature since Documentum is just one component of enterprise infrastructure and its ability to integrate with other components facilitates the overall management and deployment of infrastructure.

The following figure illustrates the security components specific to users. We will see later that **permissions** are tied to objects and form the core of **object security**. Permissions indicate what can be done to an object by different users. On the other hand, restrictions can be placed on users, irrespective of the specific objects that they may want to interact with. **Privileges** are tied to users and are enforced by the Content Server. **Client capabilities** are also tied to users but they are *optionally* enforced by Documentum client applications. Both privileges and client capabilities are attached to the user representation and stored within the repository.

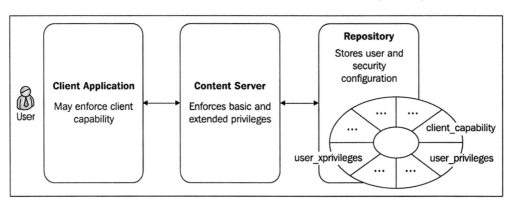

There are two important objects in a Documentum repository that store configuration information influencing various aspects of the Documentum platform:

- **Repository configuration** (type dm_docbase_config): A repository configuration object contains configuration information about a repository. Each repository must have a single repository configuration object whose object name matches the name of the repository. It provides configuration information related to security, default user for running lifecycle actions, and other repository-specific aspects.

- **Content Server configuration** (type `dm_server_config`): A server configuration object contains information that a Content Server uses to define its operation and operating environment, such as the number of allowed concurrent sessions, maximum cache sizes, the storage area locations, and the locations of executables that the server calls. There is one server configuration object per instance of Content Server serving a repository.

These objects and their relevant properties will be discussed at various points in the rest of the book.

Users

The term **user** is typically used in one of two ways—a *human* interacting with a system or the *representation of identity* within the system. The representation of identity within the system may or may not correspond to a real human user. Such accounts are typically referred to as *generic*, *system*, or *application* accounts. A user is represented as an object of type `dm_user` within the repository.

Authentication

Typically, a user *logs into* an application to authenticate the claimed identity. For example, WDK applications such as Webtop and Web Publisher challenge a user with a login screen for authentication. The user selects the repository to be accessed and presents an identity as a login/password combination. The information identifying a user for the purpose of authentication is called **credentials**.

Once the credentials are submitted, the Content Server verifies these credentials using one or more of the following ways:

1. OS (Operating System) account: This is the default authentication mechanism. The Content Server uses an internal program to match the credentials against the OS accounts. It is also possible to use a custom program to perform authentication against the OS. In this mechanism, the password is not stored in the repository.

   On UNIX systems, Content Server uses the `dm_check_password` program for OS authentication. EMC also provides the source code for this program, which can be customized to meet any specific authentication requirements.

2. LDAP (Lightweight Directory Access Protocol) server entry: The Content Server contacts an LDAP server to authenticate the credentials against an entry present in the LDAP server. LDAP is a technology used for security implementations such as central authentication and authorization.

3. In-line password: The Content Server matches the provided password against a password stored in the repository. The dm_user object has a property named user_password for storing in-line passwords. The appropriate dm_user object is identified by the login (and potentially domain) and the password is compared against the user_password property of that object.

4. Authentication plug-in: An authentication plug-in may be used, which takes over the responsibility of authentication. This mechanism provides freedom to use external authentication sources such as eTrust SiteMinder and RSA Access Manager.

The following figure illustrates these various sources against which the Content Server may authenticate a user:

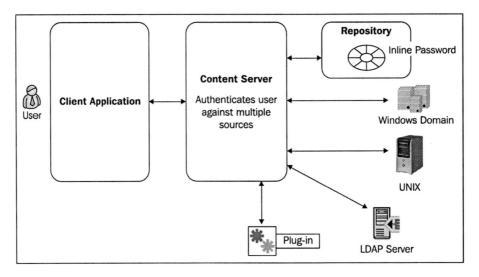

 By default, the Content Server runs in **no-domain-required** mode, which is indicated by a blank in the auth_protocol property of dm_docbase_config (the repository configuration object). In this case, users don't need to specify a domain and usernames must be unique in the repository.

On the other hand, if the Content Server is running in **domain-required** mode, the auth_protocol property is set to domain-required. In this case, multiple users can have the same name as long as they have different domains. Further, users are required to specify a domain name for authentication.

The Content Server determines the method of authentication based on the user_source property of the dm_user object. The values of this property and their implications are as follows:

User Source	Implication
LDAP	Authentication through an LDAP server. This requires at least one LDAP config (dm_ldap_config) object to be present in the repository. Documentum supports several LDAP sources such as iPlanet Directory Server, Oracle Internet Directory, and Microsoft Active Directory.
unix only	Authentication using UNIX.
domain only	Authentication against Windows domain.
unix first	Authentication against UNIX first; if that fails, authentication against Windows domain.
domain first	Authentication against Windows domain first; if that fails, authentication against UNIX.
inline password	Authentication against the password stored in user_password on the dm_user object.
plug-in identifier	Authentication with the plug-in identified by the identifier (such as dm_netegrity, which represents eTrust SiteMinder authentication plug-in).

An **LDAP configuration object** (type dm_ldap config) stores configuration for the Content Server to use for interacting with an LDAP server. For example, it contains the host name and port number of the LDAP server, information about the structure of the directory tree, and credentials for connecting to the LDAP server.

There can be multiple LDAP configuration objects in a repository but one Content Server uses only one LDAP configuration object (identified by dm_server_config.ldap_config_id) at any given time.

An LDAP configuration object can be created through Documentum Administrator or through DQL. Creation and modification of an LDAP configuration object requires Superuser privileges. Privileges are discussed later in this chapter.

Special Users

There are two special users in a repository. They are as follows:

- **Installation owner**: Installation owner is the OS account that was used for installing the Content Server.

- **Repository owner**: The repository owner is the *database owner* (DBO) of the underlying database for the repository.

Both of these users automatically get Superuser privilege in the repository. Privileges are discussed later in this chapter.

Authorization

Recall that authorization pertains to controlling access to functionality. User-specific authorization can be enforced by the client applications as well as the Content Server. Client applications utilize a user's client capability to enforce access control for functionality within the client application. They can also utilize roles to manage access to functionality within the applications. Roles are discussed in *Groups and Roles* (Chapter 6).

On the other hand, Content Server utilizes basic and extended privileges to enforce access control. As we will see in later chapters, Content Server also enforces object security in addition to these privileges.

Client Capability

The `client_capability` property of `dm_user` stores the **client capability** level. This information is available for all users, but it is up to the client applications to utilize this information for enforcing additional access control.

Documentum's client applications such as Webtop and Desktop assign specific meanings to these capabilities. These capabilities are hierarchical in the sense that one level can also imply another level. There are four levels of client capability:

1. Consumer: Consumer can search, view, and copy documents and forward tasks in workflows. This is the default capability.

2. Coordinator: The coordinator capability includes consumer capability. In addition, a coordinator can create cabinets, workflows, and virtual documents and can view hidden objects.

3. Contributor: The contributor capability includes coordinator capability. In addition, a contributor can create documents and folders, modify regular documents and virtual documents (including checkin and checkout), and delete documents.

4. System Administrator: The system administrator capability includes the contributor capability. In addition, a system administrator can manage Content Server, repository, and users and groups.

 Note that client capabilities only allow what a user can *attempt* to do within a client application. These attempts are further subject to the Content Server scrutiny using privileges and object permissions. For example, suppose that a user has coordinator client capability but no privilege for creating a cabinet. In this case, the user will not be able to create a cabinet.

Basic Privileges

While client capabilities may be enforced by a client application, privileges are enforced by the Content Server. A user's **basic privileges** are set in the user_privileges property of dm_user. These privileges are enforced by the Content Server irrespective of the client application involved.

Basic privileges are represented as integer values as follows:

Privilege	Value	Description
None	0	None of the basic privileges. This is the default value.
Create Type	1	Can create custom object type.
Create Cabinet	2	Can create, modify, and delete cabinets.
Create Group	4	Can create, modify, and delete groups.
Sysadmin	8	Can perform basic administration tasks.
Superuser	16	Can perform all administration tasks.

Unlike client capability, privileges are not hierarchical and each privilege needs to be specified explicitly. Multiple basic privilege values can be combined by adding the corresponding integer values. Thus, if we want to grant Create Type and Create Cabinet privileges to a user, the user_privileges property needs to be set to 3 (=1+2).

While the first four privilege values are straightforward, Sysadmin and Superuser privileges need some elaboration. A user with Sysadmin privilege has following features:

1. It has lower privileges as well (Create Type, Create Cabinet, Create Group).
2. It can activate/deactivate a user.
3. It can manipulate users and groups.
4. It can grant and revoke the lower privileges to other users.
5. It can create or modify system-level permission sets.
6. It can administer full-text indexing and repository.
7. It can manage lifecycles.
8. It can manipulate workflows.

On the other hand, a user with Superuser privilege has the following features:

1. It has Sysadmin privileges as well.
2. It can grant and revoke Sysadmin and Superuser privileges.
3. It can delete system-level permission sets.
4. It can become owner of all objects in the repository.
5. It can unlock checked out documents.
6. It can manipulate others' custom types.
7. It can manipulate others' permission sets.
8. It can register and unregister others' tables.

Extended Privileges

Each user also gets extended privileges, which pertain to **audit trails**. Auditing is a very important feature of the Documentum platform since it enables tracking of different types of events, which can be used later for diagnostic or research purposes. Each occurrence of an audited event is recorded as one object of the type `dm_audittrail`. Note that only the events configured to be audited generate audit trail entries.

A user normally does not get any privileges related to audit trails. The extended privileges are set in the user_xprivileges property of dm_user and can be a combination of one or more of the following:

Ext Privilege	Value	Description
None	0	No audit privileges. This is the default value.
Config Audit	8	Can configure auditing.
Purge Audit	16	Can remove audit trail entries.
View Audit	32	Can view audit trail entries.

Extended privileges are also combined by adding the corresponding integer values. For example, granting View Audit and Purge Audit results in the value 48 (=16+32).

User Management

As mentioned earlier, a user is stored in the repository as an object of type dm_user. No user can be authenticated against a repository without the presence of the corresponding dm_user object. Some important properties of dm_user are described below:

Property	Label	Description
user_state	State	Active or Inactive; only active users can connect to the Content Server. 0 means that the user can log in. 1 means that the user cannot log in. 2 means that the user is locked. 3 means that the user is locked and inactive.
user_name	Name	Display name.
user_login_name	User Login Name	Login ID or user account. This is the name used for authenticating the user.
user_login_domain	User Login Domain	Windows domain or LDAP config name.
user_source	User Source	As described earlier.
description	Description	Any free-form information about the user.
user_address	E-mail Address	User's email address.
user_os_name	User OS Name	User's OS name, if any. This property is useful when the user source is OS.

Property	Label	Description
user_os_domain	Windows Domain Name	Windows domain of the user.
home_docbase	Home Repository	Default repository for the user, useful when a user is a member of multiple repositories. Prior to Documentum release 5.3, repository was known as Docbase.
restricted_folder_ ids	Restrict Folder Access To	This property is used to restrict access to only a certain set of locations (cabinets or folders) within the repository. Note that when a folder is included, its subfolders are implicitly included in the set.
default_folder	Default Folder	Default folder for objects created by this user.
user_db_name	DB Name	User's name in the underlying database.
user_privileges	Privileges	As described earlier.
user_xprivileges	Extended Privileges	As described earlier.
client_capability	Client Capability	As described earlier.
workflow_disabled	Workflow Disabled	This property can be used to prevent a user from participating in workflows.
failed_auth_ attempt	Turn off authentication failure checking	Setting this property to -1, disables the counting of unsuccessful authentication attempts. If not disabled, this property is reset to 0 on a successful login.

User management involves creation and modification of dm_user objects. Sysadmin or Superuser privilege is required for creating a user in the repository. If the client application enforces client capabilities, then system administrator client capability is also required for this purpose. User administration also involves managing group memberships for users, which is discussed in *Groups and Roles* (Chapter 6).

Note that even though user_source identifies where a user is authenticated, the existence of the user at that source is not a prerequisite for the creation of the user in the repository.

For example, a user may be created in the repository with the default authentication set to OS, even though the user account does not exist on the OS. The user will be created in the repository although authentication attempts by such a user will fail until the corresponding user has been created at the specified source.

The users in a Documentum repository can be created in several ways:

1. The easiest way to create individual users is through Documentum Administrator. The web-based interface provides friendly ways to specify values for various user properties. For example, repository locations can be browsed and suitable values for user sources can be selected from a drop-down interface.

2. If the enterprise infrastructure already has an LDAP user directory, users can be created in the repository by using the LDAP directory as the user source. An LDAP Sync job is available that can read user information from the LDAP directory to create the corresponding user objects in the repository automatically.

3. When users need to be created frequently or if the user information is available from sources other than an LDAP directory, user creation can be scripted using DQL or API.

4. Custom application interfaces can be created using DFC and WDK for user administration tasks. This approach can also be used for importing user information from external sources of such information.

User information can be modified as well using the above mechanisms.

Help—Some DQL Queries

Here are some helpful queries related to users. These queries are based on the information presented in this chapter.

The following query retrieves some basic information about a user with login name jdoe:

```
SELECT user_name, user_login_name, user_address, description,
                                home_docbase, user_state
FROM dm_user
WHERE user_login_name = 'jdoe'
```

The following queries set up a new user named Jane Doe. The first query creates the user object. The second query creates a folder in the repository and the third one sets this new folder as the home folder for the new user.

```
CREATE dm_user OBJECT
  SET user_name         = 'Jane Doe',
  SET user_login_name   = 'jdoe',
  SET user_address      = 'jdoe@doquent.com',
  SET user_group_name   = 'docu',
  SET user_source       = 'inline password',
```

```
    SET user_privileges   =   2,
    SET client_capability =   4

CREATE dm_folder OBJECT
    SET object_name       =   'jdoe',
    SET owner_name        =   'Jane Doe'
    LINK '/Home'

UPDATE dm_user OBJECT
    SET default_folder    =   '/Home/jdoe'
    WHERE user_login_name =   'jdoe'
```

The following query lists the inactive users in the repository:

```
SELECT user_name, user_login_name
FROM dm_user
WHERE user_state = 1
   OR user_state = 3
```

The following query lists the privileges for the same user. Recall that both the basic and extended privileges are stored as numbers that are sums of the component privileges. For example, a privilege value 6 (= 2 + 4) implies Create Cabinet and Create Group privileges.

```
SELECT user_name, user_privileges, user_xprivileges
FROM dm_user
WHERE user_login_name = 'jdoe'
```

The following query lists the LDAP configuration objects present in the repository:

```
SELECT object_name
FROM dm_ldap_config
```

Documentum Product Notes

User administration is typically done through Documentum Administrator. Repetitive or batch user administration activities can be scripted using DQL or API.

Checkpoint

At this point you should be able to answer the following key questions:

1. What is user authentication? What are the different ways in which Documentum supports authentication?

2. What is authorization? What are the different ways in which Documentum supports authorization specifically for a user?

3. What is the difference between privileges and client capabilities?

4. What are the different ways for creating and managing users?

Test Your Understanding

1. Authentication and authorization are one and the same (True/False).

2. For every user with OS as user source, dm_check_password is used for authentication (True/False).

3. In the following user sources, the user account must exist in the source before the corresponding user can be created in the repository:

    a. Windows OS

    b. UNIX OS

    c. LDAP

    d. None of the above

4. The database owner for the repository database is called the installation owner (True/False).

5. The client capabilities are always enforced by client applications (True/False).

6. One of the basic privileges allows document creation (True/False).

7. Create Cabinet implies Create Type privilege (True/False).

8. Superuser implies Sysadmin privilege (True/False).

9. A user cannot create another user unless the logged-in user has system administrator client capability (True/False).

10. In order to prevent a user from authenticating against the repository, the user can be deactivated (True/False).

6

Groups and Roles

In this chapter, we will explore the following concepts:

- Groups
- Roles and Domains
- Group management

Authorization

In the last chapter, we introduced the concepts of authentication and authorization. For correct authentication each user must be identified uniquely. However, it is very common that multiple users play the same business role in an organization and need similar levels of access. If access is granted to each user separately, it may become difficult to manage the access control due to the following reasons:

1. There are a large number of users and/or resources to be secured.
2. All the users with similar access levels need to be assigned new permissions.

For example, a department may have 100 employees, where all the users need similar access levels to a set of documents. Configuring the same access repeatedly for 100 users is inefficient. Further, if this access needs to be changed (or taken away) for all of these users, it requires the same laborious process again.

Both of these scenarios lead to repeated work of the same kind that deserves to be *automated* and *simplified*. A **group** provides this capability by representing a set of users who need to be treated as equals from some perspective of authorization. **Roles** and **domains** are special types of groups that can be used by client applications to implement access control. In order to distinguish among groups, roles, and domains, the following notation will be used:

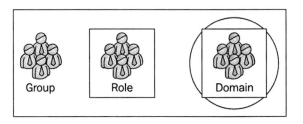

Groups

A **group** is a set of **members** where a member can be a user or another group. Thus, groups contained in other groups can provide implicit memberships. For example, suppose a group `Managers` contains a user `Sam` and another group `Executives` as members. Further, `Executives` contains `John` as a member. Implicitly, `John` is a member of `Managers` as well. The following figure illustrates this example:

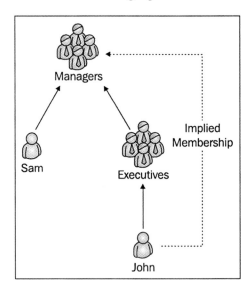

Within the repository, a group is represented as an object of type dm_group. There are three types of groups—group, role, and domain. A regular group is identified by group_class = 'group'. The other types of groups are discussed later in this chapter.

Some important properties of dm_group are described below:

Property	Label	Description
group_name	Name	Name of the group.
description	Description	Free-form description of the group.
is_private	Is Private	Indicates if the group is private or public; T means private, F means public. Public and private groups are discussed later in the section *Group Management*.
group_address	E-mail Address	Email address for the group.
group_class	Class	The type of group—group, role, or domain.
group_admin	Administrator	Name of user or group who can modify this group.
owner_name	Owner	Name of user or group who owns this group.
users_names		Names of the directly contained users in this group.
i_all_users_names		List of all users in this group, and indirect members via nested group membership.
groups_names		Names of groups that are members of this group.
i_supergroups_names		Name of the group and all groups that contain this group.
is_dynamic	Dynamic Group	Indicates if the group is dynamic; T means dynamic, F means standard.
is_dynamic_default	Treat users as members / Treat users as non-members	Determines whether the members of the dynamic group are considered members by default; T means members, F means not members.
alias_set_id	Alias Set	Object ID of an alias set associated with this group. Alias sets are discussed in detail in the chapter *Aliases* (Chapter 13).

A group can be a **dynamic group** if the members of the group can be changed when the group is being used at run time. However, the membership changes cannot be arbitrary. The dynamic behavior only allows the membership to be changed within a set of pre-configured members. There are two additional options for dynamic groups — consider members to be *members by default* or consider them to be *non-members by default*. During run time, a client can programmatically add and remove members from a dynamic group.

An example will help clarify these concepts. Suppose Sam, John, and Jane are members of Managers, which is a dynamic group. Also the members are to be considered non-members by default. When a client application checks membership of Managers, it appears to be an empty group. The client application can then add Sam, John, and Jane to Managers but no other user/group could be added. The dynamic membership of the group only lasts for the user session. In a new session, the same behavior repeats again.

Group Management

Group management involves creation, modification, and deletion of groups. The key considerations around group management are as follows:

1. Who can create groups?
2. How can groups be created?
3. What are the constraints on group creation?
4. What is the default behavior on creation of a group?

The user account used for performing group management requires Create Group privilege. The applications that enforce client capability (such as Documentum Administrator) require System Administrator capability for such a user. Now let's see the answers to our questions.

A group can be created in one of several ways — manually through an application such as Documentum Administrator or Webtop, programmatically using DFC, or by importing from an LDAP server. The LDAP Sync job, described in *Users and Privileges* (Chapter 5), can import groups as well as users from an LDAP server. The job connects to the LDAP server and retrieves users and groups according to the information stored in the LDAP configuration object.

A group's name needs to be unique in the repository, unlike users who can share the same name if they belong to different domains.

A group can be **private** or **public**. This property is available for client applications to utilize for showing or hiding groups appropriately for different users. When enforced, a public group is visible to all users and a private group only to the group owner and group administrator. Content Server does not use this property in any special way. When a sysadmin or superuser creates a group, it is public by default; otherwise, it is private by default.

Two special users (or groups) are associated with a group—**group owner** (owner_name) and **group administrator** (group_admin). The group owner is a user or group that owns this group. Group administrator is a user other than owner and superuser who can modify this group. An owner or administrator for a group can be assigned by a superuser only. When a group is created, the creator becomes the group owner, by default. A group administrator is not assigned automatically.

Roles

As mentioned earlier, there are two special kinds of groups—roles and domains. This difference is identified by the value of the group_class property. A **role** is a group with the group_class property set to role.

Roles and domains are intended to enable access control within applications to a more granular and specific level than what client capability provides. For example, Webtop gives priority to roles over client capability. Further, custom roles can be created and used in Webtop via customization. As with client capability, roles and domains have meanings to client applications only and the Content Server does not assign any special meaning to them.

Roles can form an **inheritance hierarchy** similar to an object-oriented inheritance hierarchy. When a role is added to another role, the member role is called a **sub-role** or **derived role**. The containing role is called the **parent role** or the **base role**. The sub-role is said to **inherit** from the parent role. This relationship is similar to the group membership relationship described earlier. The following figure illustrates a role hierarchy:

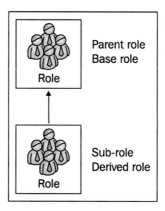

Domain

A group is identified as a **domain** when the value of the property `group_class` is `domain`. The purpose of a domain is to identify all the roles that apply to an application and, therefore, the members of a domain are roles. Once again, a domain only has meaning for client applications and not for the Content Server. Usually, one domain group is created per application. The client application only uses roles that are members of its domain.

Help—Some DQL Queries

Some helpful queries related to groups are described in this section. These queries are based on the information presented in this chapter.

The following query retrieves information about a group named `interviewers`:

```
SELECT group_name, group_address, owner_name, group_admin
FROM dm_group
WHERE group_name = 'interviewers'
```

The following query retrieves the names of the groups that a user named `dmadmindev` is a member of, directly or indirectly (through nested group memberships):

```
SELECT group_name
FROM dm_group
WHERE ANY i_all_users_names = 'dmadmindev'
```

The following query retrieves the names of the users and groups that are direct members of a group named `admingroup`:

```
SELECT users_names, groups_names
FROM dm_group
WHERE group_name = 'admingroup'
```

The following query retrieves the names of all the roles present in the repository:

```
SELECT group_name
FROM dm_group
WHERE group_class = 'role'
```

Documentum Product Notes

Group administration is typically done through Documentum Administrator. Repetitive or batch group administration activities can be scripted using DQL or API. User and group administration also involves managing group memberships where users and groups can be added to other groups or removed from them.

Checkpoint

At this point you should be able to answer the following key questions:

1. What are groups? What purpose is served by groups?
2. What are dynamic groups?
3. What are roles and domains? What purpose do they serve?
4. What are the different ways of creating and managing groups?

Test Your Understanding

1. Which of the following statements are correct:
   a. Every role is a group
   b. Every group is a role
   c. Every domain is a group
   d. Every role is a domain

2. Any user can be added to a dynamic group at run time programmatically (True/False).

3. The Content Server gives preference to roles over client capability (True/False).

4. If a user is a member of a role, it implies that this user is also a member of its sub-roles (True/False).

5. The Content Server prevents private roles from being accessible to everyone (True/False).

6. A group created by a user with only Create Group privilege can not become public (True/False).

7. The following group property identifies the kind of group:
   a. `class`
   b. `class_group`
   c. `group_class`
   d. none of the above

8. The owner and administrator for a group are one and the same (True/False).

9. Two groups can have the same name in a repository as long as they are different kinds of groups (True/False).

10. Typically, one domain group represents all the roles that will be used by an application (True/False).

7

Object Security

In this chapter, we will explore the following concepts:

- Basic and extended object permissions
- Creation and assignment of permission sets
- Object owner and superusers
- Folder security

Security—A Recap

In previous chapters, we studied various features of Documentum security including users, groups, roles, domains, authentication, client capabilities, and basic and extended privileges. These aspects focus primarily on the identity of the user. The other side of security concerns is the resource being accessed, i.e. an object. The object security defines access restrictions applied at the object-level granularity.

This chapter introduces the concepts associated with object security and how these concepts relate to other security parameters for specifying the overall access control configuration for Documentum.

The object security applies to objects of type `dm_sysobject` or one of its subtypes. All discussion in this chapter assumes the objects to be of this type unless stated otherwise.

Object Permissions

Each object in the repository is associated with permission settings that grant specific permissions to certain users and groups. These permissions are categorized into **basic** and **extended permissions**.

Basic Permissions

Basic permissions relate to accessing and manipulating an object's content and metadata and include the following levels:

Level	Value	Description
NONE	1	No access is allowed.
BROWSE	2	View metadata (properties).
READ	3	View the associated content.
RELATE	4	Create relationships, such as between annotations and PDF files, documents, and lifecycles. Documentum uses various types of relationships to manage content effectively.
VERSION	5	Create new version.
WRITE	6	Modify without changing version (modify properties without checkout or modify and check in as same version).
DELETE	7	Delete the object.

The basic permissions are hierarchical in nature implying that a particular permission level includes all the lower permission levels as well. For example, granting VERSION permission to a user will implicitly grant RELATE, READ, and BROWSE permissions as well.

Extended Permissions

Extended permissions allow specific actions against objects and support alias resolution, business rule enforcement, and ability to purge without being able to read or modify content. As we will see later, the majority of the extended permissions are useful for enforcing business rules using lifecycles. The extended permissions are as described:

Level	Description
Change Location	Move the object from one folder to another.
Change Owner	Change the owner of the object (the object owner is described later in this chapter).
Change Permission	Change the permission settings of the object (assigning the permission set is described later in this chapter).
Run Procedure	Execute a Docbasic procedure. A Docbasic procedure is one way to execute code, which may be needed for a job, workflow, or an operation in a lifecycle.
Change State	Change an object's lifecycle state.
Extended Delete	Only delete (separate from the basic DELETE permission and does not imply any other permissions).

Note that the extended permissions are independent of the basic permissions and must be granted separately and individually (i.e. they are not hierarchical). These permissions are also optional. It is possible to have an object with no extended permission specified for it.

It is important to keep in mind that one type of security access may be restricted by another. We have already seen that client capabilities and privileges may both be required to perform certain actions. Similarly, an extended permission may be insufficient on its own to perform the desired action and may also need additional basic permissions due to the effect that the action has on the object. The following table lists the dependencies of the extended permissions on the basic ones:

Extended Permission	Additionally Required Basic Permissions
Change Location	Moving from primary folder requires WRITE permission.
	Moving from non-primary folder or linking only requires BROWSE permission.
	Copying requires READ permission.
Change Owner	WRITE
	Object owner and superuser are exempt from this requirement.
Change Permission	NONE
Run Procedure	NONE
Change State	NONE
Extended Delete	NONE

The primary folder for an object is the first folder it was linked to. If the object is moved from this folder, the primary folder is the folder to which the object was linked earliest among the currently linked folders. The primary folder object ID is present in i_folder_id[0] property.

Special Users

There are two special types of users who implicitly get certain permissions—*object owners* and *users with Superuser privilege*. Ordinary users (other than these two types) must be granted specific permissions for them to be able to access the object in the desired manner.

Object Owner

Each object is associated with a user or group, which is referred to as its **object owner**. The object owner is special as far as the particular object is concerned and gets the following permissions on this object automatically:

1. READ permission

2. All extended permissions except Extended Delete

Usually, the object owner is assigned higher permissions through the applied permission set. Permission sets are discussed later in this chapter.

Managing Object Ownership

An object can only have one specified owner (dm_sysobject.owner_name) at a time, which can be a user or a group. By default, the user creating the object becomes the owner of that object. Object ownership can be reassigned to another user or group. If a group is made the object owner, each member of that group (direct or nested) is treated as object owner.

We have already seen that changing ownership relates to the extended permission Change Owner. Only a user satisfying at least one of the following requirements can change object ownership:

1. Be the current object owner

2. Have the Superuser privilege

3. Have WRITE permission and Change Owner extended permission

If the new owner is a group, then the user performing the change is required to meet one of the following conditions in addition to the conditions mentioned earlier:

1. Have the Superuser privilege

2. Be a member of the group that will become the new owner

Superuser Permissions

A user with Superuser privilege automatically gets certain permissions. A superuser is treated like an owner for *all* objects in the Documentum repository. Thus, a superuser gets the same permissions as those of the owner if no other permissions have been granted explicitly.

Permission Sets (ACLs)

So far we have seen the basic and extended permission levels. In order for the permissions to be assigned to an **accessor** (user or group), they need to be placed inside a **permission set**. A permission set (also known as **ACL** or **Access Control List**) is simply a set of basic and extended permissions associated with different accessors.

A permission set is stored as an object of type `dm_acl`. Permission sets are used for controlling access only to the objects of type `dm_sysobject` (or any of its subtypes). The valid operations on renditions are controlled by the permission set on the primary object. Recall that renditions cannot be edited or checked out.

There are four categories of accessors that can be granted permissions in a permission set—*owner* (`dm_owner` is the alias for owner), *specific users*, *specific groups*, and *world* (`dm_world` is the alias for `world`). These categories are intended to be able to resolve the permissions of any user who may attempt to access an object. The object owner is special, as described earlier. The permissions specified for the owner in the permission set can expand the permissions for the owner, but cannot restrict them to fewer than what the owner is automatically entitled to. So, specifying NONE basic permission for the owner will still let the owner BROWSE and READ the object.

Specific users and groups can be granted basic and extended permissions. Any user who is neither an owner nor included in the users and groups specified in the permission set gets the permissions granted to world.

A permission set always contains specific permissions for owner and world and may contain permissions for other accessors. A sample permission set is shown in the following figure:

Permission Set		
Accessor	Basic Perm	Extended Permission
Owner	DELETE	
John	VERSION	
Managers	WRITE	Change State
World	READ	Change Location

Resolving Permissions

It is possible for a user to be granted different permissions within a permission set. For example, a user may be the owner as well as a member of a group present in one of the permissions. Every user is implicitly a member of world as well. When this happens, the user gets all the different basic and extended permissions granted in different ways. The following example illustrates this concept:

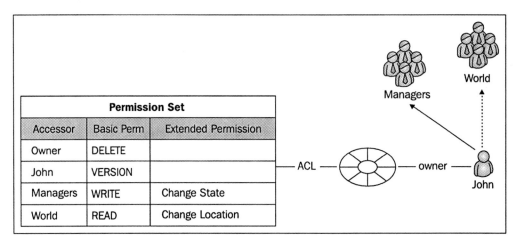

In this example, John gets permissions in four ways—as the owner of the object, as a specific user, as a member of a specific group, and as an implicit member of **World**. So what are his effective permissions? In the basic permissions, he gets DELETE, VERSION, WRITE, and READ, which means that he gets DELETE since that implies the other basic permissions. As an owner he gets all the extended permissions other than Extended Delete, so that's what he keeps since Change State and Change Location are already included.

Managing Permission Sets

A permission set is uniquely identified by a name (dm_acl.object_name) and an owner name (dm_acl.owner_name). Of course, it can also be identified by its object ID. The name of the permission set can be NULL, but the combination of name and owner must be unique within the repository if it is not NULL.

Creating Permission Sets

Any user can create a permission set, though applications (such as Webtop) honoring client capabilities would require System Administrator capability for this purpose. Depending upon the nature of the creator, permission sets are categorized as **system permission sets** or **user permission sets**.

A system permission set is created and modified by a user with Sysadmin or Superuser privileges. Such a permission set is owned by the repository owner (dm_dbo) and is available to all the users of the repository.

A user permission set is created by any user without Sysadmin or Superuser privileges. Such a permission set is owned by the creator and is available only to the owner.

Some key properties of a permission set are described as follows:

Property	Label	Description
r_is_internal	Is Internal	T indicates that this is a custom permission set (explained later in this chapter), F indicates otherwise.
acl_class	Class	Regular (0) means private for the owner, Public (3) means available to everyone. The values 1 and 2 are used with permission set templates, which are discussed in *Aliases* (Chapter 13).
object_name	Name	Name of the permission set.
owner_name	Owner	Owner of the permission set.
r_accessor_name		Repeating accessor names.
r_accessor_permit		Repeating basic permissions.
r_accessor_xpermit		Repeating extended permissions.

The r_accessor_* properties describe the individual permissions. These are repeating properties and their values at the same index correspond to each other. For example, r_accessor_name[3] = 'Joe', r_accessor_permit[3] = 4 means that Joe is being assigned RELATE permission. Refer to the table under Basic Permissions, discussed earlier in the chapter, for the numeric values of basic permissions.

Extended permissions have an additional aspect that multiple extended permissions can be assigned to one accessor. The Content Server translates the multiple extended permissions into a single internal integer code and this one integer value is stored per accessor.

Assigning Permission Sets

Permission sets are reusable and one permission set can be assigned to multiple objects. Each object sharing the same permission set grants the same permissions to the same users, with the exception that the owner may be different for each of these objects.

When an object of type `dm_sysobject` (or one of its subtypes) is created, the Content Server automatically assigns it a permission set according to certain rules. A permission set is assigned to an object by setting `dm_sysobject.acl_name` = `dm_acl.object_name` and `dm_sysobject.acl_domain` = `dm_acl.owner_name` properties. Each Content Server instance has a default ACL configuration (`dm_server_config.default_acl`), which specifies the rules for assigning a permission set to a new object.

A server configuration object (`dm_server_config`) contains information that a Content Server uses to define its operation and operating environment, such as the number of allowed concurrent sessions, maximum cache sizes, or the default ACL mode. The server configuration object is discussed in *Users and Privileges* (Chapter 5).

The rules for assigning a permission set to a new object are described below:

Default ACL	Value	Description
Folder	1	The primary folder's permission set (`dm_folder.acl_name`) is assigned to the object.
Type	2	The permission set configured for the object's type (`dmi_type_info.acl_name`) is assigned to the object.
User	3	The default permission set for the creator of the object (`dm_user.acl_name`) is assigned to the object. This is the default setting.

An object can have only one permission set assigned to it at any time, but it can be reassigned a different permission set subject to any of the following conditions:

1. The user performing the reassignment is the object owner.

2. The user performing the reassignment has Superuser privilege.

3. The user performing the reassignment has `Change Permission` extended permission.

While the user and system permission sets are reusable, there are *ad hoc* permission sets as well, which are called **custom permission sets**. A custom permission set is created by the Content Server when permissions assigned to an object are modified.

 Essentially a custom permission set is intended for one-time use and is not reusable. When the permissions for an object are modified, the Content Server creates a new permission set with the resulting permissions and assigns it to the object. The Content Server names the custom permission sets starting with dm_45.

The Custom permission sets are also created when permission set templates are used; this process is discussed in *Aliases* (Chapter 13).

Folders and Permission Sets

Just like other sysobjects, each folder (and cabinet) is also assigned a permission set. This permission set is used for two purposes:

1. Controlling access to the folder object
2. Assigning to the objects that have this folder as their primary folder when the server's default ACL mode is set to `folder`

A folder's permission set does not restrict access to the objects linked to it unless the **folder security** is enabled for the repository.

The folder security can be used for securing folders by adding restrictions based on links to the folders. When folder security is in use, object security is necessary, but not sufficient for adding documents to or removing documents from a folder. When folder security is enabled, a WRITE permission is required on the folder to link (create, import, copy to) or unlink (move, delete) content within it. Appropriate object permissions are still required for the operation to succeed. Other operations can be performed on the content with the BROWSE permission on the folder.

Folder security is configured by setting dm_docbase_config.folder_security = 1. By default, folder security is enabled and it can be changed by users with Superuser or System Administrator privileges. Folder security can be configured using Documentum Administrator, DQL/API scripts, or via DFC.

Help—Some DQL Queries

Some helpful queries related to object security are described in this section. These queries are based on the information presented in this chapter.

The following query retrieves basic permissions granted on a given object:

```
SELECT r_accessor_name, r_accessor_permit
FROM dm_acl
WHERE object_name =
  (SELECT acl_name
    FROM dm_document
    WHERE r_object_id = '0900006480000509')
AND owner_name =
  (SELECT acl_domain
    FROM dm_document
    WHERE r_object_id = '0900006480000509')
```

Note a few things in this query. DQL doesn't allow joins when retrieving repeating properties (accessor name and permit)—this query achieves the same effect using subqueries. Also note that both acl_name and acl_domain should be checked when looking up the ACL for an object.

It is not straightforward to check extended permissions through queries since they return an integer value that needs to be decoded. It is best to view extended permissions through an application such as Webtop or Documentum Administrator.

The following query retrieves the ACL information for the type dm_document:

```
SELECT acl_name, acl_domain
FROM dmi_type_info
WHERE r_type_name = 'dm_document'
```

Note that this may be empty since it is optional for a type to have an associated ACL.

The following query retrieves the ACL information for a folder named Temp:

```
SELECT acl_name, acl_domain
FROM dm_folder
WHERE object_name = 'Temp'
```

The following query retrieves the ACL information for a user named dmadmindev:

```
SELECT acl_name, acl_domain
FROM dm_user
WHERE user_name = 'dmadmindev'
```

Documentum Product Notes

The Administration node in Webtop or Documentum Administrator can be used for creating and managing permission sets. The permissions tab on object properties can be used for reassigning a permission set or for modifying permissions. System Administrator client capability is needed for these operations.

Trusted Content Services (TCS) is an optional component of Documentum architecture and requires a separate license to use with the Content Server. It provides enhanced security features such as encrypted communication (SSL) and storage, electronic signatures, and additional restrictions in addition to the usual object security.

Checkpoint

At this point you should be able to answer the following key questions:

1. What is a permission set and how is it different from a permission?
2. What are basic permissions? What are extended permissions?
3. How is a permission set selected to be assigned to a new object?
4. What is a custom permission set? Who can create it and why is it needed?
5. How does folder security provide additional object security beyond the permission sets?
6. What kind of security is provided by Trusted Content Services?

Test Your Understanding

1. A user with Extended Delete permission automatically gets WRITE permission as well (True/False).
2. A permission set can contain multiple ACLs (True/False).
3. The VERSION permission implies the following permissions:
   a. WRITE
   b. READ
   c. BROWSE
   d. DELETE
4. The object owner automatically gets all the extended permissions (True/False).

5. A permission set created by a user without Sysadmin or Superuser privilege is called a custom permission set (True/False).

6. The default ACL mode for the server is set to folder. A user creates an object in folder A and then moves it to folder B. The final permission set on the object is the same as:

    a. The permission set of the user

    b. The permission set of the type of the object

    c. The permission set of the folder A

    d. The permission set of the folder B

7. The same object from question 6 is now linked to folder C as well. The permission set of the object:

    a. Changes to the permission set of folder C

    b. Remains unchanged

    c. Changes to the permission set of the owner

    d. Changes to the permission set of the type

8. Folder security can be used to control the following:

    a. Who can link an object to a folder

    b. Who can delete an object linked to a folder

    c. Who can version an object linked to a folder

    d. The default permission set for the objects created in the folder

9. Jane is the owner of an object. The permission set allows Extended Delete for world. As a result, Jane has the following extended permissions:

    a. Change location

    b. Change owner

    c. Change state

    d. Extended delete

10. The ACL domain for a sysobject is the same as:

    a. The name of the assigned ACL

    b. The owner of the assigned ACL

    c. The set of basic permissions in the assigned ACL

    d. The set of extended permissions in the assigned ACL

Part 3

User Interface

Searching

8
Searching

In this chapter, we will explore the following concepts:

- Simple and advanced searching with Webtop
- Saving searches
- Full-text indexing
- Subscription

Locating Objects

The previous chapters showed how to create and modify objects in the repository. We saw that various mechanisms could be used for this purpose including programming and interactive scripts using IAPI or IDQL. However, the most common mechanism of interacting with the repository remains applications, particularly Webtop.

The same can be said about locating documents or, more generally, objects within the repository. Webtop provides one of the easiest available interfaces for accessing content within the repository. Typically, consumers of information are quite business savvy and the alternatives to Webtop for searching documents are less desirable to them.

There are two key ways of locating objects within the repository:

1. *Navigating* through the browser tree to a known path
2. *Searching* using the words that may be found within the metadata or content

The navigation mechanism is used when the user knows (or can guess) where an object is located within the folder hierarchy. This chapter is about locating objects by searching for them without knowing where they may be linked within the folder tree. Since Webtop is the most common way to perform these searches, this chapter will focus on Webtop functionality related to searching. Further, only the classic view of Webtop will be discussed and used for illustration.

Search Process

Webtop enables searching for objects in two ways and there are some nuances to each approach that we will explore in this chapter. However, there is a common underlying pattern to the search process either way.

Webtop allows the following sequence of steps for searching, though some of these steps are optional (refer to the figure for a better understanding):

1. Specify the search criteria: The **search criteria** define the conditions that an object has to satisfy to be a part of the results. Search criteria typically include words being searched for in metadata or in content and additional conditions (such as last modification date being later than a specified date) on the metadata. The criteria may be explicitly specified by the user, may be implicit, or could be retrieved from a previously saved search.

2. Submit the search request: The search request is submitted once all the desired criteria have been specified.

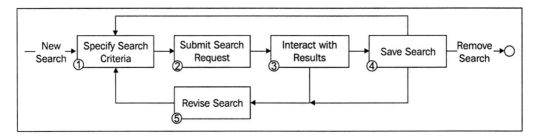

Webtop passes on the search request to the Content Server where the search is performed. Searching includes matching within content if full-text indexing (described later in this chapter) is enabled in the deployment.

3. Receive results and interact with them: The Content Server always honors the configured security and will not return objects for which the current user has only NONE permission. Webtop receives the results and presents them to the user in a paginated manner.

The user can interact with the results by navigating through pages and can perform operations on individual objects by selecting them.

4. Revise search: If the user feels that the search criteria need to be altered to get better results, the search can be revised. Revising a search takes the user to the advanced search screen with the current criteria populated on the form. The user can alter the search criteria and can submit the request again.

5. Save search: Finally, if the user wishes to reuse the search criteria later, there is an option to save the search. At a later time, the user can initiate step 1 from an existing saved search. The saved search can also be revised or removed.

This interaction pattern remains the same, though there are some variations with the two types of searches and the optional aspects. The rest of this chapter addresses these variations and details.

Simple Search

Simple search is simple in terms of what the user has to do to perform the search. There is just one field to specify the search words (criteria) and a button to submit the search request. The biggest benefit of simple search is that the user just specifies the search words and gets to the results quickly. This is how it looks on the screen:

Since version 5.3 of Documentum, objects in multiple repositories can be queried for one search operation. For a simple search, all repositories designated as *default* are searched. Multiple repositories can be set as default using preferences, as described later in this chapter.

A search operation can query full-text indexes as well as object properties. Full-text indexes capture information about the text contents of documents and enable searching the content as well as the object properties. The full-text indexes are created by the Index Server when it is present as a part of the Documentum installation.

The simple search request is processed in different ways depending on whether full-text indexing has been enabled.

Search—without Full-Text Indexing

When full-text indexing is not enabled, simple search is truly simple. The searches are case sensitive, meaning that the search words are matched exactly as specified. Words separated by spaces are ANDed, meaning that if two words are specified both must be present in the match. The search words are matched against the values of the following properties: `object_name`, `title`, and `subject`.

Search—with Full-Text Indexing

Full-text indexing makes the simple search more powerful and a little bit more complex. With full-text indexing, simple search behavior changes as follows:

1. The search is now case insensitive, meaning lower-case letters are considered a match with upper-case letters as well.

2. The space-separated search words are ORed, meaning that if any word is matched the target object is considered a match.

3. All searchable properties are compared for a match. A property is searchable if `is_searchable` is set to `1` for this property in the data dictionary. The data dictionary is discussed in *Custom Types* (Chapter 9).

4. The indexed content is also searched for matches for the search words.

5. The search words can include `*` as **wildcard**. A wildcard is a pattern that can match anything. An `*` matches any text of any length. For example, `te*` will match `ten`, `test`, and `temporary` as well.

 Note that with or without full-text indexing, a phrase can be searched for by enclosing it in double quotes, as in "out of the box".

Advanced Search

Advanced search provides full flexibility to the user for specifying the search criteria. The user can reach the advanced search screen (shown in the following screenshot) when initiating a new search or when revising the last executed search. The biggest benefit of advanced search is that the user can be very specific about the search criteria and is more likely to get relevant results, particularly when there is a large number of potential matches for the search words.

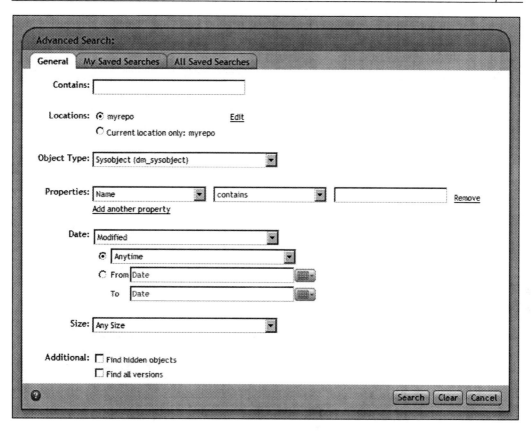

Advanced search enables the user to be very specific about the search criteria in the following manner:

1. Additional areas can be specified to be included in the search besides default repositories. Including additional areas may require re-authentication against the new areas, if the authentication credentials have not been saved. *Login preferences* can be used to cache login credentials to avoid re-authentication at such times.

2. Specific locations—folder paths and cabinets can be used for the search rather than searching the entire repository.

3. If **EMC Documentum Enterprise Content Integration Services (ECIS)** is installed, external sources other than Documentum repositories can also be included in the search (ECIS is described later in this chapter).

4. Date-based conditions can be included in search criteria. For example, search all documents that were last modified after 2nd May, 2007.

5. The target object type can be specified for the search. For example, perform the search only against objects of type `my_report`, where `my_report` is a custom type.

6. The file size can be used in the criteria. For example, find all documents with the content size larger than 2MB.

7. Hidden objects can be included in searches.

8. All versions can be searched rather than only the current ones.

9. Multiple property conditions can be specified as a part of the criteria. Each property condition is of the form *name–operator–value*. For example, subject–begins with–Medicine.

    The properties available to be used in these conditions are dependent on the selected object type. The different property conditions can be combined together using AND and OR operators.

Interacting with Results

The results from a search request, simple or advanced, are shown in the **content pane**. The content pane is the area in Webtop other than the header, footer, and left navigation. For practical purposes, the content pane can be considered the *main area* of the screen.

The result objects are shown as a list in the content pane and pagination is available if the result list size is more than the number of items displayed on one page. When page navigation (shown in the next screenshot) is enabled, users can go from one page to an adjacent page, jump to a specific page, or jump to the first or the last page.

If the size of the result list is very large, Webtop may start showing results before the processing is complete. In this case a message – "**Processing...**", appears in the header indicating that more results may be arriving.

This message is a hyperlink to a **Search Status** page. The search status page shows the status of the search request in terms of each source – a repository or an external source. The status information includes *source, status, number of results,* and a *message*. This screen also allows the search to be stopped.

The search results screen allows the search to be revised through a **Revise Search** link, which takes the user back the **Advanced Search** screen that displays the parameters for the current search.

It is also possible to save a search from the results page and this capability is discussed next.

Saving Searches

Once the user has performed a search, the user may want to save the search for running again in future. This may be a desirable choice when a particular search is performed frequently or when the search criteria contain several conditions. Either way, a saved search can be run again by clicking a hyperlink.

When a search is saved, it is the search criteria that are saved and not the search results. Therefore, the same saved search can return different results when run at different times. For example, if a saved search lists all patient reports in the system the result list can be different after more reports have been imported into the repository. The search is saved as a *hidden* dm_smart_list object in the *home_cabinet*/Saved Searches folder. dm_smart_list extends dm_sysobject and has no properties of its own.

Webtop stores the search criteria as XML in **smart lists**. Documentum Desktop uses DQL to store the search criteria in the smart lists. Therefore, the saved searches are not compatible across different applications.

Here is the screenshot displaying the **Saving Your Search** option:

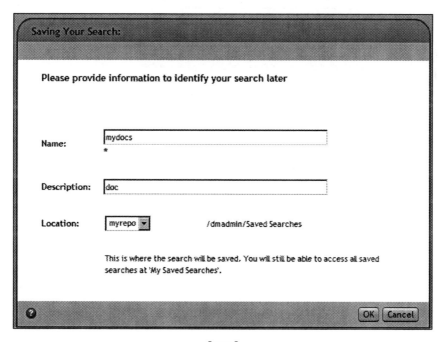

For saving a search it is possible to specify a destination repository, if multiple repositories are available. If the user saving the search has Superuser privilege, the search is saved as a **global saved search,** which is available to all users. Otherwise, this search is saved as a **personal saved search,** available only to the user saving it.

Saved searches can be accessed through two categories:

1. **My Saved Searches**: This includes only the personal saved searches.
2. **All Saved Searches**: This includes both personal and global saved searches.

These tabs appear on the **Advanced Search** screen and have similar layout—each shows a list of saved searches. For each saved search three actions are available:

1. **Remove**: removes the saved search
2. **Edit**: loads the search criteria in the Advanced Search screen
3. **Submit**: submits the search criteria saved in the search and shows the results

Here is the screenshot displaying the **My Saved Searches** option:

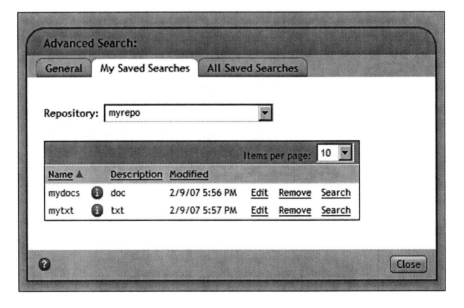

Let's now see how the **All Saved Searches** option looks like:

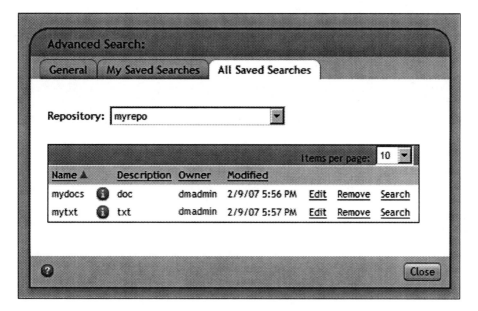

Search Preferences

Preferences in Webtop allow users to store their preferred ways of interacting with the application, so that they can avoid specifying these choices repeatedly. Essentially, preferences help users to work efficiently. Search preferences are the preferences that affect search behavior for a user.

The search preferences allow users to specify the desired search behavior in the following ways:

1. **Columns** specify the set of properties that are displayed in the search result, as shown in the following screenshot:

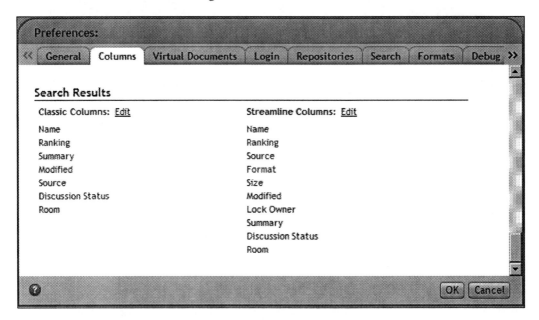

2. Favorite repositories indicate the repositories a user accesses frequently. New repositories can be added to this list by providing information about new connection brokers. The newly added repositories stay in the **Favorites** list only for the duration of the current user session.

    In order to keep these additional repositories permanently available even after the session expires, the connection brokers need to be added to the dmcl.ini file on the application server that hosts Webtop.

3. Default search locations are included in searches without the need for specifying them explicitly for each search, as shown:

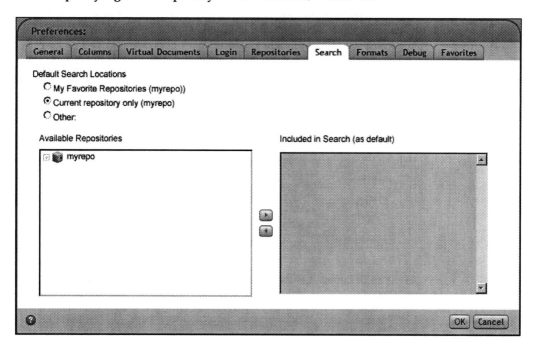

Full-Text Indexing

We have already seen that full-text indexing affects the search in significant ways. It is worth understanding the fundamental concepts of full-text indexing even though it is an optional component of the Documentum platform.

Full-text indexing is implemented by the **Index Server**, which is an optional component. One Index Server can provide indexing for multiple repositories and, thus, multiple Content Servers. An **Index Agent** is associated with a Content Server and supports the indexing needs of the associated repository.

The Index Server participates both in creation of and searching of the full-text indexes. Full-text index creation is coordinated by the Index Agent through the FAST Index Plugin (see the note about FAST in *Documentum Product Notes* later in this chapter). Querying the indexes is coordinated by the Content Server using the FAST Query Plugin. This is shown in the following figure:

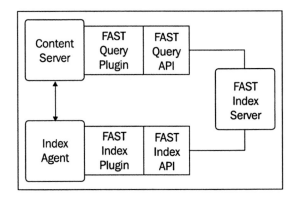

The Index Server receives requests for indexing when a sysobject undergoes one of the following operations:

- save

- saveasnew

- checkin

- destroy

- branch

Only those sysobjects are indexed that have their a_full_text property set to TRUE. There is a configurable delay between saving the changes and indexing of metadata and content.

Due to the delay between saving changes and indexing modified or new content, there is a period during which searches may not retrieve results based on the latest changes. Once the modified objects are re-indexed, the latest changes start showing up in the search results.

Once the Index Server indexes an object (metadata and content), it stores the index information in dm_fulltext_index objects in the corresponding repository. The indexes are associated with the repository that contains the object being indexed.

Frequently Accessed Objects

Searching and navigation provide convenient ways to locate objects based on criteria or location, respectively. However, if there are certain documents that a user accesses frequently, these approaches are still somewhat inefficient. Webtop provides two mechanisms for accessing such objects quickly—subscriptions and shortcuts.

Subscriptions

Subscriptions represent bookmarks, favorite locations, or favorite documents. Users can subscribe to the objects or paths that they access frequently. All the subscribed objects show up under the **Subscriptions** node in Webtop.

Objects can be subscribed to or unsubscribed via the **Tools | Subscribe** and **Tools | Unsubscribe** menu items in Webtop.

A user can also subscribe to **notifications** for events on objects. By default the checkin event for an object generates notifications. Other events can also be configured for notification. Notifications can be subscribed and unsubscribed by using **Tools | Turn on notification** and **Tools | Turn off notification** respectively.

Subscriptions and **Inbox** are shown in the following figure:

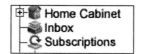

Notifications show up in the user's **Inbox** in Webtop.

Shortcuts

Shortcuts provide quick access to objects. Subscriptions can be seen as *shortcuts within Webtop*, where the users can jump to the documents directly without having to go through the folder structure or a search.

True shortcuts provide direct access to objects from outside the Webtop. Once the user tries to follow the shortcut, he/she may have to log into Webtop. A shortcut can be created in one of the following ways:

1. Using the menu item **File | Email as Weblink**. This creates an email message with the shortcut to the item embedded as a hyperlink.

2. Using drag and drop on the shortcut icon from the properties tab. This approach can be used to create a shortcut on the Windows desktop.

3. A shortcut can also be stored as a bookmark in the browser.

Once a shortcut has been created, it can be followed by selection or double-clicking to access the object. The object will be accessed via Webtop and the user may be required to authenticate again.

When accessing an object through the shortcut, the user gets the option to *view* or *edit* the object. If the shortcut was to a non-current version of the object, the user gets the option to *access the current version* instead. As always, appropriate permissions are still needed to access the object.

Help—Some DQL Queries

While this chapter focused on searching using Webtop, the DQL SELECT query is also used to perform searches. We have already seen SELECT queries in several chapters, so we will only look at the full-text support in DQL queries here. The following queries assume that an Index Server is present in the Documentum deployment.

While various aspects of full-text searches are supported in DQL, we will look at the following key aspects:

1. The SEARCH clause enables searching the full-text index.

2. The keywords SCORE and SUMMARY can be used in the selected values list:

   a. The SCORE keyword returns the document's *relevance ranking* as determined by the Index Server. A higher relevance ranking implies a better match. By default, the results are returned in descending order of SCORE.

   b. The SUMMARY keyword returns a summary of each document as determined by the Index Server.

The following query retrieves documents containing the word hiring in their content or metadata:

```
SELECT object_name, SCORE
FROM dm_document
WHERE SEARCH DOCUMENT CONTAINS 'hiring'
```

The following query retrieves documents containing the word hiring, or firing, or both in their content or metadata:

```
SELECT object_name, SCORE
FROM dm_document
WHERE SEARCH DOCUMENT CONTAINS 'hiring firing'
```

The following query retrieves documents containing the phrase "hiring process guidelines" in their content or metadata:

```
SELECT object_name, SCORE
FROM dm_document
WHERE SEARCH DOCUMENT CONTAINS '"hiring process guidelines"'
```

Note that * can also be used as a wildcard in the search string.

Documentum Product Notes

The search behavior can be altered by the presence of **Enterprise Content Integration Services (ECIS)**. ECIS is an optional component of the Documentum platform and it allows external sources of information (such as databases, websites, or other enterprise applications) to be searched along with the Documentum repositories.

EMC provides adaptors for various external data and content sources so that they can also be searched through ECIS. For example, one search request can pull results from two repositories, a database, and Google and show all the results together. If ECIS is not installed, the external source options are not available for searching.

Full-text indexing is implemented by the Index Server, which is also an optional component of the Documentum platform. However, the Index Server license is included with the Content Server license. EMC embeds FAST InStream in the Index Server, by default. Typically, the Index Server uses significant CPU and memory resources and is deployed on a separate physical server.

Full-text search behavior can be configured via the dfcfull.properties file, which is present in the $DOCUMENTUM/config (or %DOCUMENTUM%\config on Windows) directory. For example, the maximum number of results returned by any query can be restricted with the following entries:

```
dfc.search.maxresults=1000
dfc.search.maxresults_per_source=350
```

See *Architecture* (Chapter 4) for additional notes on the Index Server.

Checkpoint

At this point you should be able to answer the following key questions:

1.   What is the difference between simple and advanced searches in Webtop?

2.   What is full-text indexing? How is it enabled? What is the impact of the full-text indexing on search behavior?

3.   How can sources other than Documentum repositories be searched from within Webtop?

Test Your Understanding

1.   A document `AprReport.pdf` is linked to only one folder—`JohnsDocuments`. Jane has only NONE permission on `JohnsDocuments` but BROWSE permission on `AprReport.pdf`. Which of the following statements are true within Webtop?

     a.   Jane can use the browser-tree to navigate to `AprReport.pdf`

     b.   Jane can use simple search to locate `AprReport.pdf`

     c.   Jane can use advanced search to locate `AprReport.pdf`

     d.   None of the above

2.   A document `AprReport.pdf` has the following metadata: `subject='money'`, `title='April Report'`, and `keywords[0] = 'finance'`. The report document itself contains the word `'Boston'`. The Index Server is not installed. Which of the following statements are true?

     a.   A simple search for `'finance'` can find `AprReport.pdf`

     b.   A simple search for `'Apr'` can find `AprReport.pdf`

     c.   A simple search for `'Money'` can find `AprReport.pdf`

     d.   A simple search for `'Boston'` can find `AprReport.pdf`

3.   A document `AprReport.pdf` has the following metadata: `subject='money'`, `title='April Report'`, and `keywords[0] = 'finance'`. The report document itself contains the word `'Boston'`. Full-text indexing is enabled. Which of the following statements are true?

     a.   A simple search for `'finance'` can find `AprReport.pdf`

     b.   A simple search for `'Apr'` can find `AprReport.pdf`

     c.   A simple search for `'Money'` can find `AprReport.pdf`

     d.   A simple search for `'Boston'` can find `AprReport.pdf`

4. An attempt to revise a search takes the user to:

   a. Simple Search screen

   b. Advanced Search screen

   c. My Saved Searches screen

   d. All Saved Searches screen

5. A user with the following privilege can create a global saved search:

   a. Create Global Search

   b. Sysadmin

   c. Superuser

   d. Config Audit

6. A saved search returns the same results every time it is run (True/False).

7. A search saved in Desktop can be run from Webtop (True/False).

8. Subscribing to a document sends an email to the user every time the document is checked in (True/False).

9. A shortcut to a Documentum object when placed on Windows desktop also stores the object locally (True/False).

10. If a user receives a shortcut as a Weblink in email, he or she is guaranteed to be able to access the linked object (True/False).

Part 4

Application Development

Custom Types

DocApps

Workflows

Lifecycles

9

Custom Types

In this chapter, we will explore the following concepts:

- Managing custom types
- Data dictionary

Custom Types

Documentum provides a large number of built-in object types that support the functionality of the platform. Some object types are general purpose and can be used for business purposes as well. However, all possible business needs can neither be anticipated nor supported by default. Therefore, Documentum allows creation of new object types, which are called **custom types**. This chapter addresses creation and management of custom types.

 Before reading this chapter, it would be helpful to revisit *Objects and Types* (Chapter 3) since the majority of the concepts pertaining to object types apply here as well. The concepts repeated here are explained in more detail in Chapter 3.

Managing Custom Types

A user-defined object type is called a **custom type** and the user-defined properties are called **custom properties**. Properties are also known as **attributes**. Custom types can be created, modified, and removed as long as certain rules are followed. This section describes the detail around managing custom types.

Creating a Custom Type

A custom type can be created using Documentum Application Builder (DAB), using Documentum Administrator (DA), or using DQL/API scripts. DAB is the most commonly used application for creating custom types since it fully supports the *data dictionary* (see *Data Dictionary* later in this chapter) and it has a Graphical User Interface (GUI) specifically designed for creating and managing custom types.

Further, DAB can also be used for packaging the types into a *DocApp* (DocApps are described in detail in Chapter 10). The following screenshot shows the DAB screen for creating and updating a custom type:

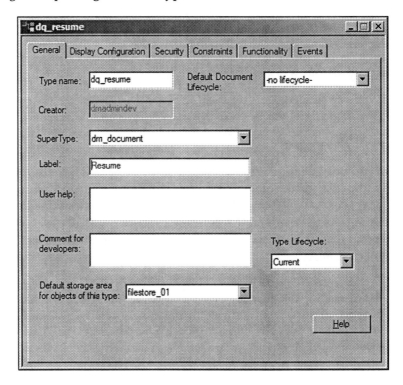

DA provides basic support for managing custom types. For example, DA does not provide an interface for defining value assistance for a property. The following screenshot shows the screen for creating and updating custom types in DA:

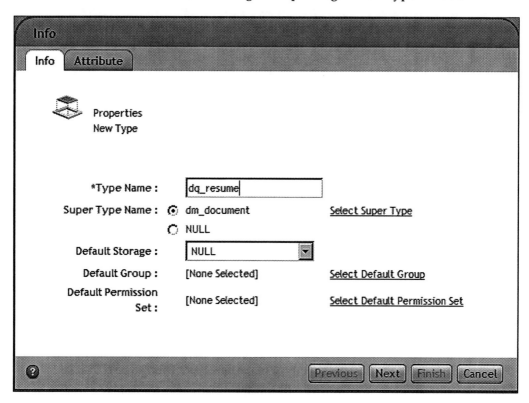

Creating a custom type is a privileged operation and only the users with following privileges can do so:

- Create Type
- Sysadmin
- Superuser

The user creating the type becomes the owner of the type.

A custom type can extend an existing type through inheritance (see *Type Hierarchy* in Chapter 3). A new custom type can have an existing custom type or one of the sets of Documentum object types as its supertype. The most common supertype for a new custom type for representing documents is dm_document.

It is also possible to create a custom type without a supertype. Such a type is called a **NULL** type. Only a user with Superuser privilege can create a NULL type. A NULL type is useful for storing data that does not need the usual object management features such as versioning. There are several built-in types that are NULL types such as dm_user, dm_session, and dm_alias_set. If a custom type is intended to only store non-versionable data, a NULL type may be appropriate for this purpose.

Recall that any given type uses up to two tables (one for single-valued properties and one for repeating) of its own for storing non-inherited properties of its objects. There are additional views for retrieving all the properties together.

The following key information is needed or captured in DAB when creating a new custom type:

Info	Description
Name	Name of the type. A type name must be unique (case-insensitive) in the repository and can be up to 27 characters long. The additional constraints on the type name are that it cannot contain a space or punctuation nor can it be same as any DQL reserved word, such as SELECT or WHERE.
	Further, it cannot start with dm_, dmi, dmr_, a number, space, or a single quote. It is recommended that a custom prefix be used for custom type names to distinguish them from the other types.
Creator	The user creating the type.
Supertype	The supertype of the new type. This can be NULL.
Label	User-friendly version of the name, for display purposes in Documentum client applications.
Default Lifecycle	A lifecycle that can be attached to a document of this type, without identifying the lifecycle explicitly.
Default Storage Area	A **storage area** identifies where the content files are stored for objects. The default storage area identifies where the content files for objects of this type will be stored by default.
Default Permission Set	The default permission set is used when the default ACL mode (see Chapter 7) for the Content Server is set to Type. In this case, a new object of this type gets this permission set.
Template Document	One or more **template documents** can be created for the type, which are available to users when they are creating a new object of this type. The template documents are stored in the Templates cabinet in Documentum repository.

Events for Types

An **event** is an operation on an object or something that happens in an application. A **system event** is an event that is recognized and is auditable by the Content Server. For example, checkin on a particular document in a system event. Promoting or demoting an object in a lifecycle is also a system event.

On the other hand, an **application event** is recognized and is auditable only by the application. The application events can be defined using DAB. For example, an application event can be used to hold off workflow activities based on external dependencies such as conditions in other systems.

Suppose that a workflow activity requires a performer to review a document. However, the performer needs access to data in another system in order to complete this task. An application event can be sent to the performer's inbox to trigger the activity once the required data is available in the other system.

The following screenshot displays the DAB screen for managing application events:

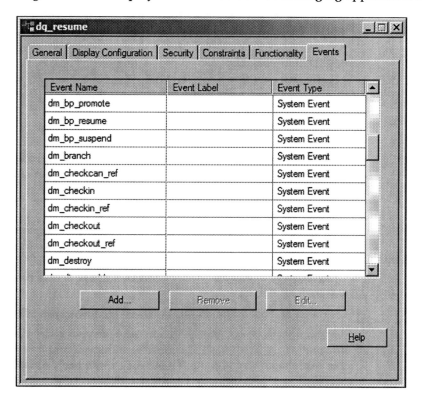

Note that events are also inherited from supertypes just like properties. The events shown in the previous screenshot, are inherited from dm_document — these are system events and cannot be modified or removed.

Properties

An object type inherits all the properties of its supertype. Custom properties can be created for custom types, with each property being defined in the following manner using DAB:

Info	Description
Name	The name of a property must be unique within the type, including inherited properties. The property should be named in all lower case letters and 'select', 'from', and 'where' are not valid names. Further, a property name cannot start with dm_, a_, i_, r_, a number, a space, or a single quote.
Label	User-friendly version of the name, for display purposes in Documentum client applications.
Data Type	The data type of the property constrains the types of values this property can take. The allowed data types are integer, boolean, string, double, time, and ID.
Length	Length of the property if the data type is string.
Repeating	Whether this is a repeating property or single-valued.
Default Value	Default value for this property.
Input Mask	The **input mask** is used for validation and provides a pattern for valid values for this property. The mask is specified using the following characters with special meaning in addition to the regular characters: #: A numeric digit 0-9 A: An alphanumeric character including a-z A-Z 0-9 &: Any ASCII character ?: Any alphabetical character a-z A-Z U: Similar to ? but automatically converted to upper case before saving L: Similar to ? but automatically converted to lower case before saving For example, suppose that an account number consists of 8 characters where the first three characters must be alphabetic and the remainder can be alphanumeric. An input mask for this property can be specified as ???AAAAA.

The following screenshot shows the DAB screen for managing a custom attribute:

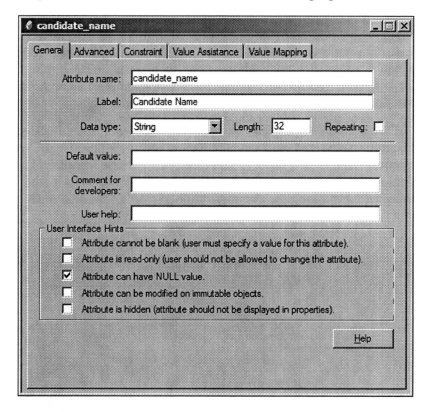

Search Support for Properties

Some information about properties can be provided to support the user interface for searching on this custom type.

Info	Description
Searchable	Whether this property is searchable
Default Search Value	Default value for the search field for this property
Allowed Search Operators	The types of matching that can be done on this property for searching, such as =, <>, 'begins with', etc.
Default Search Operator	Which search operator among the allowed ones should be selected by default

Displaying Properties

Client applications can utilize **display configurations** to display properties for different object types in different ways. Display configurations are created using DAB. Documentum Desktop (also known as Documentum Desktop Client) and WDK applications utilize display configurations extensively. WDK applications such as Webtop use display configurations to include custom properties in the standard interface without writing any additional user interface code.

For example, Webtop can display custom properties in an editable form on a separate tab on the properties page using a display configuration. The following screenshot shows creation of a **Display Configuration** named **Resume**. When the properties of an object of type dq_resume are viewed in Webtop, a separate tab named Resume will use this display configuration to display the attributes included in it.

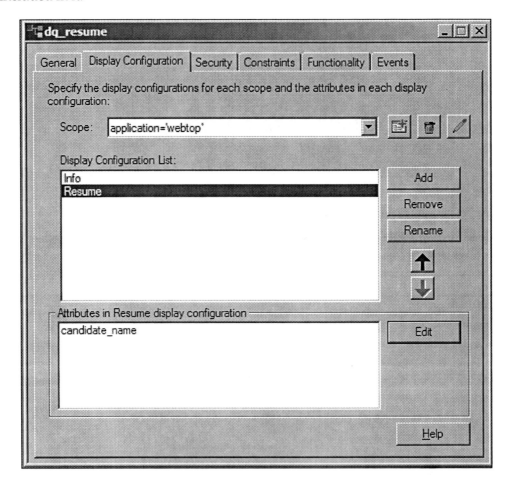

A display configuration specifies when certain properties should be displayed and how their display should be organized. Each display configuration specifies three aspects:

1. *Scope* determines when to use this display configuration. It can be a combination of an application and a role, implying that this configuration should be used when the specified role is accessing an object of this type in the specified Documentum application. Thus, even within the same application it is possible to create different views of the same object for different roles.

2. For each scope, multiple *configurations* can be defined. For example, Webtop displays the configurations as tabs on the properties view of objects.

3. For each configuration, an ordered *list* of properties is specified, which constitutes the configuration. These properties are displayed together in the Documentum application.

Note that, implicitly, the properties not included in display configurations are not displayed on the application interface. Thus, display configurations can be considered as a way of exposing or hiding custom properties.

Validation

Constraints are conditions that must be met by objects and properties to be valid. For example, a custom type may represent an account with a property account ID. Then a potential constraint on this type is that the account ID property is required to be unique within the repository. Constraints for custom types can occur in the following forms:

Constraint Type	Description
Primary Key	The primary key uniquely identifies an object within the repository. There is only one primary key for a type.
Unique Key	A unique key is unique among all the objects of this type in the repository. There can be multiple unique keys for a type.
Foreign Key	A foreign key establishes a constraint between properties of two types. A Sysadmin privilege is required to create a foreign key constraint.
Check	A check constraint is a condition expressed as a Docbasic expression or a routine that evaluates to true or false.

An error message can be specified for each constraint and it can be displayed to the user when the corresponding constraint is violated. Optionally, each constraint can be flagged to be enforced in which case the client application should enforce the constraint.

The constraints can also be specified at the property level where the constraint is specified as a Docbasic expression. An error message and enforcement flag can also be specified at the property level.

Value Assistance

When users need to specify values for object properties through client applications it may be desirable, due to business reasons, to limit the values that can be specified for a property. For example, if a property represents a country name its underlying data type is string but only the country names are meaningful values for this property. When the user needs to specify a country name, the application can limit the value to one of the actual country names. This ability is supported by a feature known as **value assistance**.

Value assistance specifies a list of valid values for a property that can be used by client applications to facilitate valid user input. The list of valid values can be an explicitly fixed list or a DQL query that returns a list of appropriate values from a data source — objects or database tables. The following screenshot shows the DAB screen for managing value assistance for an attribute named experience on custom type dq_resume:

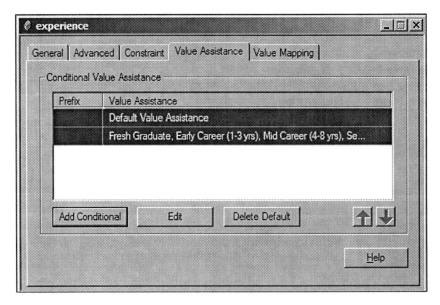

It is also possible to use one of many lists for value assistance on a property. The list to use is decided dynamically based on certain conditions. One of these lists is identified as the *default* list and the others are identified as *conditional*. Each conditional list is associated with a condition and is used when that condition is true. The default list is used when none of the conditions is true.

There are two other options that affect the behavior of these lists. One specifies whether the queries can be *cached*. Caching queries improves performance by storing the lists retrieved for value assistance. However, if the data being queried is modified, the changes are not available in the application until the cache has been refreshed.

The other option specifies whether the list of values is *complete* — this essentially specifies whether the user can enter a value other than those in the list, for example using a combo list or box. This option is useful when a set of initial or most frequently used values is known, but there may be cases when other values are acceptable but not known beforehand.

Note that value assistance cannot be specified for Boolean properties. A Boolean property can only be `true` or `false`.

Value Mapping

Another useful feature for client applications is **value mapping**. A value mapping defines a correspondence between *stored values* and *labels to display* for those values. Suppose that a property represents a color and stores the value in RGB format. In this case, a value mapping can be useful to help the user view/select an appropriate value. For example, a stored value `FF0000` may be mapped to `Red`, which makes more sense to most users.

Note that `$value` is a useful keyword that can utilize user-specified single values in a validation error message or in a value assistance query at run time. For example, `SELECT title from book WHERE author = $value(user_author) and category = $value(user_category)`. This query retrieves book titles where the author and category of the books are provided by the user.

Modifying a Custom Type

Once a custom type has been created, a need may arise to alter it. This may happen when an unforeseen need arises or the requirements change.

Modifying a custom type is a privileged operation and only the type owner or a user with Superuser privilege can modify a custom type. The default Documentum types cannot be modified.

A custom type can be modified only in the following ways:

1. The type can be dropped (removed). Dropping a type is allowed only when there are no objects of this type and this type has no subtypes.
2. A new property can be added to the type.
3. A non-inherited property can be dropped (removed) from the type.
4. The length of a non-inherited string property can be increased.

When a custom type is modified, it automatically affects its objects, its subtypes, and objects of its subtypes.

Just like objects, a type needs to be checked in after it has been modified. However, remember that a type cannot be versioned and no history of type changes is retained (other than potentially through audit trails). The type exists only in its most recent form.

It is possible to change the type of an object, though that does not change the type itself. The type of an object can only be changed to the immediate supertype or an immediate subtype of the existing type. For example:
```
change my_doc objects to dm_document WHERE object_name
= 'xyzreport.pdf'
```

Using Custom Types

Custom types can be used just like the built-in Documentum types except for the restrictions described earlier. Much of the additional information specified about custom types is stored in the data dictionary.

Data Dictionary

The **data dictionary** consists of a set of types whose objects store information about types, such as constraints for properties, default lifecycle, default property values, value assistance, mapping info, and localized text. Since the data dictionary is stored in the repository, it is available to all client applications.

Note that the data dictionary is available for the client applications to use and the Content Server does use the data dictionary for its operation.

The data dictionary information is often cached by applications. In order to refresh this cached information with new changes, the data dictionary can be **published**. The API method `publish_dd` can be used to publish the data dictionary.

Help—Some DQL Queries

Some helpful queries related to object types are provided in this section.

The following query retrieves the type of a given sysobject:

```
SELECT r_object_type
FROM dm_sysobject
WHERE object_name = 'mydoc.txt'
```

The following query retrieves all the NULL types:

```
SELECT name
FROM dm_type
WHERE super_name = ' '
```

The following query retrieves the supertype of a given type:

```
SELECT super_name
FROM dm_type
WHERE name = 'dm_document'
```

The following query retrieves the names and labels for attributes of a given type:

```
SELECT attr_name, label_text
FROM dmi_dd_attr_info
WHERE type_name = 'dm_sysobject'
```

Documentum Product Notes

DAB provides complete access to the data dictionary through type and property editors. Further, when DAB checks in changes to types, the data dictionary is automatically published.

Checkpoint

At this point you should be able to answer the following key questions:

1. What are custom types? How are they different from built-in Documentum object types?

2. What privileges are required for managing custom types? What changes are allowed to an existing custom type?

3. What is the data dictionary? What benefits does it provide?

Test Your Understanding

1. Which of the following are correct statements?

    a. A custom type can have two supertypes

    b. A custom type can be a supertype of two other types

    c. A custom type can be a supertype of dm_document

    d. A custom type can be a subtype of dm_document

2. It is desired to store invoice documents in the repository. The only specific metadata to be stored with the invoice is an invoice number. Which of the following are feasible approaches for this purpose?

    a. Store the invoices as dm_document objects and use the subject property to store the invoice number

    b. Store the invoices as dm_document objects and add a property called inv_number to store the invoice number

    c. Store the invoices as objects of a custom type invoice and add a property called inv_number to store the invoice number

    d. None of the above

3. A custom property can have the following data type:

    a. Alphabetical

    b. Alphanumeric

    c. ASCII

    d. String

4. The following privilege is required to create a NULL type:

    a. Create Type

    b. Sysadmin

    c. Superuser

    d. None of the above

5. It is desired to create a custom type `my_invoice` for storing invoice documents. It will have the following custom properties— `invoice_id` (single valued) and `account_id` (single valued). The following tables will be created for this type:

    a. `my_invoice`

    b. `my_invoice_s`

    c. `my_invoice_r`

    d. `invoice_id_account_id`

6. A custom type does not need to be checked in since it cannot be versioned (True/False).

7. Since the data dictionary is stored in the repository, the Content Server enforces type constraints for all applications (True/False).

8. The length of a custom property can represent precision for floating point values (True/False).

9. Multiple lists can be specified for value assistance on one property (True/False).

10. Suppose `my_report` and `my_invoice` have `dm_document` as their supertype. Further, `my_partner_invoice` has `my_invoice` as its supertype. There is an object of type `my_invoice`. Its type can be changed to:

    a. `dm_document`

    b. `my_report`

    c. `my_partner_invoice`

    d. None of the above

10
DocApps

In this chapter, we will explore the following concepts:

- Customizing Documentum
- Creating and managing DocApps
- Archiving and installing DocApps

Documentum Customization

Any serious business use of the Documentum platform requires **customization**. Documentum provides the model and framework for creating a business application. Documentum is designed to be customized and customization can involve aspects such as custom types, business objects, presentation, and security.

Documentum has a rich set of features and this richness brings complexity. As a result, customization of a Documentum deployment touches multiple layers of the architecture. Management of these customizations and their ongoing maintenance can become a daunting challenge. The several layers are shown in the following figure:

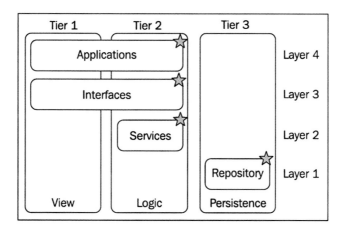

It becomes even more challenging when Documentum infrastructure is shared among different departments and each department has its own customizations. In this case, it is possible that different customizations are performed by different teams of developers but deployed within the same repository (as shown in the following figure).

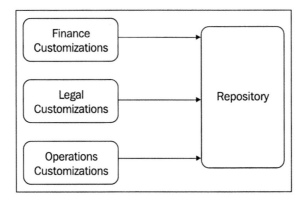

Another dimension of managing customizations is the number of environments that a customization may need to be deployed on. Customizations necessarily require at least two environments—*development* and *production* (also known as *live*). Ideally, a third environment called *QA* (or *staging*) should also be present. The development environment is used for developing the customizations and may allow uncontrolled changes.

Normally, this environment is primarily used by the developers. Once the customizations are ready to be tested, they are deployed in QA. Testing can occur in QA while development and bug fixes are taking place in development. Once the customizations reach a level of quality that is passed in QA, the customizations are deployed to production (as shown in the next figure). The challenges of managing customizations across multiple Documentum environments, in addition to the previously described concerns, would make it a huge hurdle to cross were it not for a feature called DocApp.

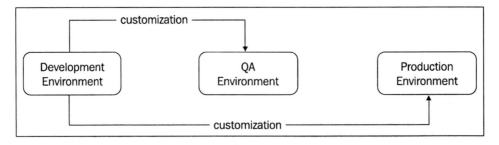

DocApps

A **DocApp** is a package of repository objects and is itself a repository object. A DocApp is stored as an object of type `dm_application` and is also referred to as an **application**. It packages other repository objects by storing *pointers* (object IDs) to those objects.

Typically, a DocApp packages types, permission set templates, repository objects, lifecycles, alias sets, and executables. Some key properties of `dm_application` are as listed:

Property	Description
`application_object_id`	Repeating property, object IDs of all objects contained in the DocApp. These are the *pointers* to the packaged objects. Many other properties relate to the individual objects and correspond to this property by respective indexes.
`app_version`	Version label for the DocApp.
`object_name`	Name of the DocApp.
`def_alias_set_id`	The object ID of the default alias set for the DocApp. This alias set contains all the aliases specified for the DocApp.

> `dm_application` is a subtype of `dm_sysobject` and its objects have tag 08 in their object IDs. Recall from *Objects and Types* (Chapter 3) that objects of `dm_document` have tag 09 in their object IDs. Further, `dm_folder` has 0b and `dm_cabinet` has 0c as its type tag.

DocApps facilitate management of a set of objects together and these objects are typically related to a customization. A DocApp should be used to package only related objects. Unrelated customizations should be packaged in separate DocApps. Typically, objects related to one application are packaged in one DocApp. For example, the Web Publisher DocApp packages all the objects required to be used with Web Publisher.

DocApps address the challenges related to customizations mentioned earlier. Since one customization may involve multiple objects, all of these objects can be managed (created, modified, reinstalled) together. A DocApp can be created in one repository and then installed in another repository, thus facilitating portability across repositories and environments. One repository can contain multiple DocApps (recall that each DocApp is an object itself). Therefore, it is a good idea to only keep objects related to one business-level customization in one DocApp.

Managing DocApps

In a typical development cycle, a DocApp is created in a development repository. When the customizations are ready to be tested, the DocApp is archived (also said to be *serialized*) onto the file-system. Then the **DocApp archive** is used to install the DocApp in a test environment.

This process is repeated until the customization is considered ready for prime time. At this point, this DocApp archive can be installed in a production repository. If the customization is a part of a product, the DocApp archive is included in the product distribution.

Creating and Modifying DocApps

DocApps are created and managed via **Documentum Application Builder (DAB)**. A Superuser privilege is required for creating a DocApp. The following screenshot shows the main screen of DAB with an open DocApp. The left pane organizes the contents of the DocApp. The status bar at the bottom shows information about the state of the connection to the repository.

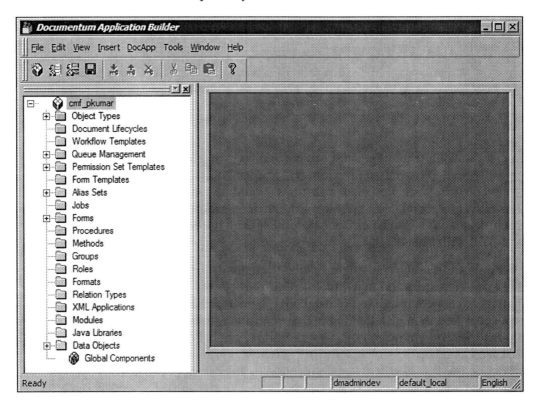

The primary purpose of a DocApp is to package objects related to a customization. DocApps are also the primary method of storing and deploying business objects. A customization may involve the following objects:

Object	Description
Custom Types	Custom types are used to store information beyond what is supported by built-in types.
Lifecycles	Lifecycles describe a sequence of states for documents based on business rules. See the chapter on lifecycles (Chapter 12) for more details.
Aliases	Aliases are important for installing the same DocApp in multiple repositories. Since different repositories can have different sets of users, groups, and locations it may not be useful to specify explicit values for this purpose in the DocApp. Aliases can provide placeholders, which are replaced with actual values at the time of DocApp installation. Aliases defined for a DocApp become a part of the default alias set for the DocApp. Aliases are useful in other ways as well and are discussed in detail in *Aliases* (Chapter 13).
Procedures	A procedure is a Docbasic
Methods	A method is code written to a specification that can be executed as needed or through a job. Methods can be written in Java or Docbasic. Along with the code, a method is also represented as a Documentum object.
Jobs	A job executes a method on a schedule. Jobs are useful for performing work periodically or on demand.
Documents	A document is an object of type dm_document or one of its subtypes.
Workflow Templates	A workflow template represents a business process and is used to create instances of that process.
Forms	Forms are used to capture user inputs in a business process.
Permission Set Templates	Permission set templates enable dynamic assignment of rights using aliases. See *Aliases* (Chapter 13) for more details on permission set templates.
Formats	A format typically describes a content structure. Formats are discussed in *Working with Content* (Chapter 2).

Since DAB is used for managing objects in a DocApp, it also lets users check in the changes to these objects. Many objects can be versioned on checkin but the following cannot be versioned: types, alias sets, permission set templates, methods, groups, data objects, XML applications, and formats and relation types.

Archiving DocApps

A DocApp resides in the repository as an object. In order to take it from one repository and install into another, Documentum supports converting it to an intermediate form. This intermediate form is a **DocApp archive**, which is the representation of a DocApp on the file system.

The sole purpose of creating a DocApp archive is to later install it into a repository and the archive can include some options that influence the installation process. The following properties of dm_application store these options. Note that the properties shown in the following table are all repeating properties—the value at each index corresponds to the object ID in the application_object_id property at the same index.

Property	Description
content_transfer_ option	Defines how to handle cabinets or folders when copying them to a target repository. It applies only to objects of type cabinet or folder.
	The valid values are:
	0: Copy all directly or indirectly contained objects
	1: Copy only the hierarchy (the directly or indirectly contained folders, but not the documents in the folders)
	2: Copy just the cabinet or folder itself, but none of its contained objects
	3: Copy only the cabinet or folder and its directly contained documents
target_loc_alias	An alias that resolves to the location (a cabinet or folder path within the repository) where an object in the application needs to be copied.
target_perm_alias	An alias that resolves to the name of a template ACL to be applied to the created object. See the chapter on alias sets (Chapter 13) for more on template ACL.
target_owner_alias	An alias that resolves to the name of the owner of the created object. The default value is the user performing the installation.
upgrade_option	Defines how to handle the object when the DocApp is upgraded (the DocApp archive is installed over an existing DocApp). In this scenario the object being installed is likely to already exist (duplicate object) in the repository.
	The valid values are:
	0: Overwrite the object
	1: Ignore (skip) the object
	2: Version the object

We will see later in this chapter that Docbasic procedures, specified as pre-install and post-install procedures, can be run by Documentum Application Installer during the installation process. These procedures are identified by a combination of the chronicle ID and version label for each of the procedures.

Recall that chronicle ID and version together can identify an object. If the pre-install and post-install procedures are specified in the DocApp, these actual procedures must also be included in the DocApp.

Property	Description
pre_install_proc_id	Chronicle ID of the pre-installation procedure
pre_install_proc_label	Version label of the pre-installation procedure
post_install_proc_id	Chronicle ID of the post-installation procedure
post_install_proc_id	Version label of the post-installation procedure

The following screenshot shows how installation options are specified for an object in DAB:

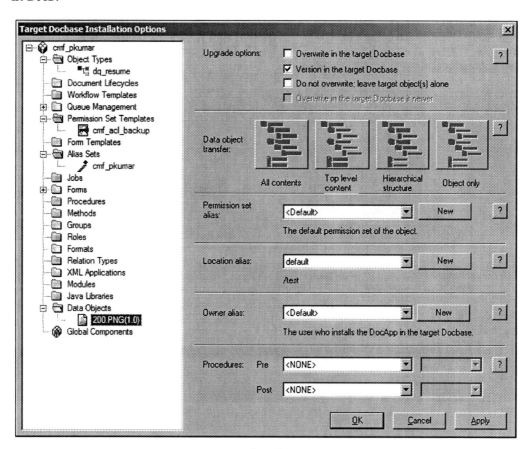

Note that if an object of a custom type is present in a DocApp, the custom type must also be included.

The DocApp is a versionable object in the repository, but its version is not stored in an archive created from the DocApp. When an archive is installed over an existing DocApp, it increments the version of the existing DocApp and merges the contents of the existing DocApp and the one being installed from the archive.

 When an object is added to a DocApp, all renditions of the object are automatically included. However, when a virtual document is added its components are not added automatically. Virtual documents are discussed in detail in Chapter 14.

Installing DocApps

Installing a DocApp is a privileged operation and it can only be performed by users with Superuser privilege. A DocApp is installed using **Documentum Application Installer (DAI)**. The main screen of DAI, just before it is ready to install the DocApp from the selected archive, is as shown:

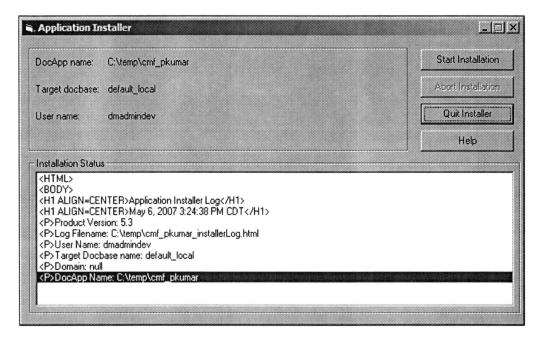

Prerequisites

A DocApp installation requires certain prerequisites to be met in order to complete successfully. The target repository for DocApp installation must contain the cabinets, folders, permission sets, and locales needed by the DocApp. Not all of these objects have to be exactly the same as present in the source repository. Some objects can be replaced via the use of aliases.

The same requirement applies for users and groups—either the same users and groups should be present or there should be corresponding users and groups with the same permissions and privileges.

The target repository can be prepared to meet the prerequisites prior to DocApp installation in several ways:

1. A pre-installation procedure can ensure that the prerequisites have been met. The procedure can create the required objects in the target repository.

2. The required objects can be included in the DocApp itself so that they are installed along with the DocApp.

3. According to installation options, the user installing the DocApp can be prompted to select alternative objects from the target repository to fulfil the needs of the DocApp.

4. The required objects can also be created manually through DA or DQL, though this is a cumbersome and error-prone option.

Installation Process

DAI follows the sequence of steps illustrated in the following figure for installing a DocApp:

Let's have a look at the steps:

1. The process begins with execution of any configured pre-install procedures.

2. The custom types are installed.

3. The aliases are resolved by prompting the user performing installation according to the configuration.

4. The objects are installed using resolved location, permission set, and owner aliases. If so configured, locations (cabinets or folder paths) for objects can be automatically created if they are missing in the target repository.

    At this point, conflicts for naming and object types are also resolved. If an object with the same name and type already exists in the repository, the object is installed as the next version of the same object.

5   Finally, the post-installation procedures are run.

Help—Some DQL Queries

Some helpful queries related to DocApps are provided in this section.

The following query retrieves the names of the DocApps installed in a repository:

```
SELECT object_name
FROM dm_application
...
```

The following query retrieves the names of sysobjects included in a DocApp named cmf_pkumar:

```
SELECT o.object_name
FROM dm_sysobject o, dm_application a
WHERE ANY a.application_object_id = o.r_object_id
AND a.object_name = 'cmf_pkumar'
```

Documentum Product Notes

Documentum Application Builder and Documentum Application Installer are desktop applications and can be installed together with the same installer. These are not WDK-based applications; they communicate directly with the Content Server.

Checkpoint

At this point you should be able to answer the following key questions:

1. What is a DocApp? What purpose does it serve?
2. How is a DocApp created and modified?
3. What is a DocApp archive? How is it created?
4. How is a DocApp archive installed into a repository? What options can modify the installation behavior? What are the prerequisites and steps in the installation process?

Test Your Understanding

1. A DocApp is stored as an object of type:

    a. dm_docapp

    b. dmi_docapp

    c. dm_application

    d. dmi_application

2. The version of a DocApp is preserved when a DocApp is archived and installed into another repository (True/False).

3. A DocApp can be created with:

    a. Documentum Administrator

    b. Workflow Manager

    c. Documentum Application Builder

    d. Documentum Application Manager

4. A DocApp can exist:

    a. On the file system

    b. In a repository

    c. In a database

    d. None of the above

5. A DocApp archive can exist:

    a. On the file system

    b. In a repository

    c. In a database

    d. None of the above

6. The following privilege allows creation of a DocApp:

    a. Sysadmin

    b. Superuser

    c. Create DocApp

    d. Create Type

7. When an object is added to the DocApp:

    a. Its renditions need to be added manually

    b. All renditions are added automatically

    c. One rendition is added automatically

    d. Renditions cannot be added to a DocApp

8. When a virtual document is added to the DocApp:
    a. All of its immediate component objects are automatically added
    b. All components are added recursively
    c. No components are added automatically
    d. Virtual documents cannot be added to a DocApp

9. When a folder object is included in a DocApp and its archive is installed in a repository:
    a. Only the folder object is added
    b. The folder object and other objects directly linked to the folder are added
    c. The folder object and all objects linked directly or recursively to it are added
    d. Any of the above based on configuration

10. The target repository must have exactly the same users and groups as were present in the repository where the DocApp was created (True/False).

11
Workflows

In this chapter, we will explore the following concepts:

- Designing workflows
- Using workflows

Business Processes

A **business process** is a set of linked activities that create value by transforming an input into a more valuable output. Both input and output can be artefacts and/or information and the activities can be performed by humans, machines, or both. The processes can serve the purpose of the core business operations (manufacturing, sales, etc.), management (strategy, planning, tracking, etc.), or support (hiring, accounting, etc.) of the core business operations.

The following figure illustrates how a candidate selection process for hiring can be automated using Documentum. The hiring process is usually a much bigger process, including activities prior to gathering resumes and following the interviews. However, this example only automates a short portion including screening and interview activities. This example will be referred to repeatedly to illustrate the concepts being discussed.

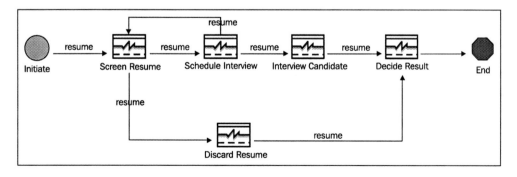

Technology offers a great potential to serve businesses by making business processes more efficient or by providing capabilities that were infeasible without the use of technology.

For example, automated business processes can make key information available faster and facilitate important decision making. Efficient execution of processes can reduce costs and improve cash flow. Since almost all business processes rely on some sort of documents, enterprise content management has a key role to play in business process management. In the hiring process example, candidate resume is a key document that affects decision making, flow, and outcome of the process.

Documentum supports process automation via workflows. There is a subtle difference between the meanings of process and workflow as far as Documentum is concerned and a good understanding of this difference can prevent any unnecessary confusion about the terminology.

In simple words, a **process** is the description (or design or definition) of how a set of linked activities are supposed to be executed and the kind of information they process. In Documentum terminology it is known as a **workflow template**. When a specific piece of information is acted upon by specific performers (humans or programs) according to the process defined by a workflow template, this execution of the process is known as **workflow**. In other words, a workflow is an instance of a workflow template.

Workflow Concepts

The difference between the design and execution of a process can be generalized in terms of the following considerations:

- *Design-time*: Design-time considerations apply when the process is being designed and modeled.
- *Run-time*: Run-time considerations apply when the process definition is in place and the process is being executed.

These differences are important for distinguishing between certain terms even though these terms are often used interchangeably.

There are a few fundamental concepts related to workflows. A **workflow template** is a process definition and prescribes how the process should be executed. A **workflow instance** (or just workflow) is a process in execution. Multiple workflows, created from the same workflow template, can execute simultaneously with each workflow processing different content items.

A workflow template consists of **activities** linked together via **flows**. A flow describes the movement of information from one activity to another. **Performers** are assigned to activities to carry them out. A workflow template is created by developers at *design time* and then *installed* into a repository for use.

When a workflow is created by end users from a workflow template, specific objects are **packaged** and passed to the **tasks** corresponding to the initial activities. As performers carry out tasks, they may alter existing objects or create new objects. These objects are passed on as packages to the following tasks. Workflows, tasks, and packages are *run-time* instances.

For example, in the hiring process described earlier, there may be resumes for two candidates — John Doe and Jane Doe. Each resume gets packaged separately and gets passed into a separate workflow instance. Each instance creates a task for **Screen Resume**. John's resume may be screened by a different performer from the performer screening Jane's resume. Let's have a look at the process:

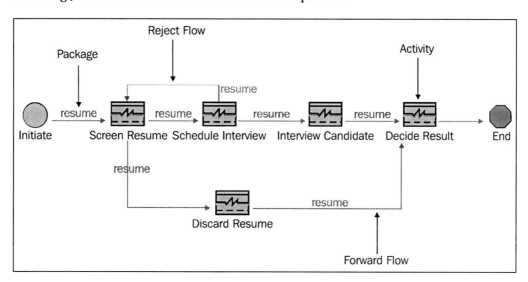

The following sections provide details of process design and execution on Documentum. It may be helpful to revisit the earlier paragraphs to regain perspective if any of the details later appear to be confusing.

Workflows and Customization

Workflows form a key component of Documentum customization. Workflow templates are usually bundled with other customization components in DocApps (See Chapter 10 for details).

A business process can be automated using Documentum in the following manner:

1. *Analyze*: The information is gathered about the business process to be automated.

2. *Model*: Each process to be automated is modeled in terms of activities, performers, flows, and packages.

3. *Define*: The model is formalized as a workflow template using Workflow Manager. The template is validated and installed in the desired repository.

 Workflow Manager is the desktop tool for visually designing workflows and is installed by the DAB installer. Business Process Manager (BPM) is a separate product that offers enhanced features for designing workflow templates.

4. *Use*: Business users with appropriate access start creating workflow instances from the workflow template. Various performers participate in these workflows.

5. *Modify*: If the process definition needs to be modified, the workflow template is uninstalled, modified, validated, and installed again.

The following sections describe the mentioned steps in more detail.

Analysis

Analysis of a business process involves gathering information regarding the activities involved, sequence of activities, whether there are any special situations and how they are handled, performers of activities and if the performers can be referred to as business roles, information and documents that are passed through activities, and if they can be modified by activities. The information gathered via analysis is used for modeling the process in a form suitable for Documentum.

In the hiring process example described earlier, analysis may require talking to the Human Resources managers and the interviewers to understand the details such as how resumes are screened, who the interviewers are, if there are timing constraints between receiving a resume and scheduling an interview, who needs to be notified if there are any issues, etc.

Modeling and Definition

Modeling and definition of processes share several aspects and are discussed together in this section to avoid repetition. Modeling maps the requirements for the business process to Documentum terminology to facilitate definition. The model is defined in a Documentum repository as a workflow template using the Workflow Manager.

A workflow template is saved as an object of type dm_process in the repository. Creating a workflow template is a privileged operation and requires coordinator capability and Sysadmin/Superuser privileges. Saving, installation, and uninstallation of a template require write permission on the template or Sysadmin/Superuser privileges.

While most of the process definition involves details about activities, performers, and flows, some aspects are specified at the workflow template level:

1. *Owner*: Initially, the creator of the workflow template is the owner but the owner can be reassigned later.

2. *Default alias set*: The set of aliases that can be used for resolution during workflow execution. See *Aliases* (Chapter 13) for more detail.

3. *Auditing*: Turning on auditing for the template enables completed workflows to be shown in workflow reports.

Let's have a look at the workflow template properties:

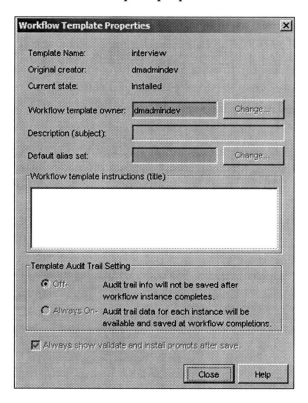

Each workflow template also has an associated **state**, which identifies where the template is in the development process. A template can be in one of the following states:

1. *Draft*: The workflow template is under development.
2. *Validated*: No process definition errors present in the template.
3. *Installed*: The template is available for instantiation (creating workflows from the template).

A newly created template is in the *draft* state. When the developer validates it successfully, its state changes to *validated*. A validated template can be installed and its state changes to *installed*. For making changes to the template it needs to be uninstalled, when it goes back to the validated state. While changes are being made to the template, it is again in the draft state. Thus, a template can move back and forth between these states but workflows can be created and be operational only while the corresponding template is in the installed state.

Activities

An **activity** is a step in the business process and a **process** consists of a set of interconnected activities. Two activities in a process can have two types of connection (direct or indirect):

1. **Serial** (in sequence): If one activity must be completed before the second can begin, they are considered to be connected serially.
2. **Parallel**: If the two activities can be carried out simultaneously, they are considered to be connected in parallel.

In the hiring process example, *Schedule Interview* and *Interview Candidate* are serial activities. If there was an additional activity called *Contact References* and it could be performed between *Schedule Interview* and *Decide Result* but either before, after, or at the same time as *Interview Candidate*, then it could be placed in parallel to *Interview Candidate*, as shown:

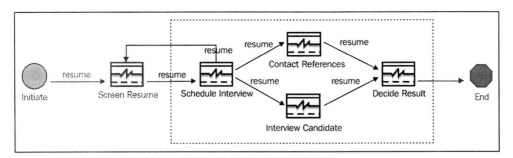

Note that in the complete figure shown earlier, **Discard Resume** seems to be in parallel to **Schedule Interview** and **Interview Candidate**. However, the business logic requires that only one of these paths be taken—either discard the resume or interview the candidate. So these paths are not truly parallel paths. However, if the resume is not discarded both interviewing and reference-checking need to happen, so they are truly parallel activities.

Each activity is stored as an instance of dm_activity. An activity can be reused across multiple workflow templates and even within the same workflow template.

However, two occurrences of the same activity cannot occur in parallel in one workflow template. Further, activities must be uniquely named in a workflow, even if there are two occurrences of the same activity within a template.

An activity can be **manual** or **automatic**. A manual activity is performed by a human user while an automatic activity is performed by a program on behalf of a user. For example, reviewing a press release document would be a manual activity while sending out a welcome email to a new employee can be an automatic activity.

In the hiring example earlier, **Discard Resume** can be an automatic activity, which moves the resume to another folder in the repository. The following screenshot shows the interface for viewing and updating activity properties in the Workflow Manager:

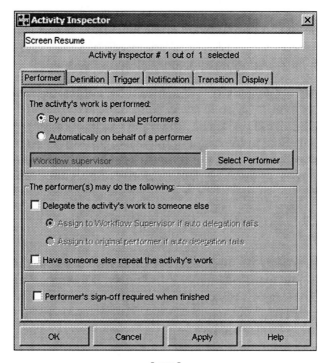

If the activity is automatic, it can be performed on behalf of one of the following users:

- Workflow supervisor—owner of the workflow, usually the user who initiated the workflow
- Repository owner
- Previous activity's performer
- Specified user

An automatic activity is performed by a **method**, which is a program conforming to certain requirements. A method can save results of its execution to a file or a server log. A method can be selected for an automatic activity only if it is a valid workflow method (tagged with *Use as Workflow Method* in DAB).

A workflow method is identified by dm_method.a_special_app='Workflow'. It can also be specified if the workflow should be halted if the method fails.

An activity can specify **conditions** for starting and completing the corresponding tasks. These conditions can be used for validation of business rules. In the hiring process example, it may be a start condition for the *Schedule Interview* activity that contact information is available for the candidate.

An activity can also be configured to *notify* the **workflow supervisor** about the progress of the corresponding task. Notifications can be sent to the supervisor's Inbox for delays in both beginning and completion of tasks.

A **priority** can be set for an activity and is useful for automated tasks. The priority can be set to *low*, *medium*, *high*, or *dynamic*. Automatic activities are executed by what is known as the workflow agent. When the workflow agent executes automatic activities, it executes them in the order of decreasing priorities—among the activities ready to be executed an activity with a higher priority is executed before an activity with a lower priority. Dynamic priority allows applications to set the priority at run time.

Performers

A **performer** for an activity is a user who performs the corresponding task (recall that a task is a run-time manifestation of an activity). If the task is automatic, it is performed on the performer's behalf (which means that the security constraints used by the program are those of this user and any changes made by the automatic task are recorded in the performer's name).

An activity can be assigned one of the following performers:

1. Workflow initiator, who is usually the workflow supervisor as well

2. Repository owner

3. Previous activity's performer

4. Specific user—explicitly selected at design time or specified as an alias, which is resolved at run time

5. All users in a group—explicitly selected at design time or specified as an alias, which is resolved at run time. All users in the group must complete the task for the workflow to move forward.

6. Single user from a group—all users in the group are notified but the first one to acquire the task from his/her *Inbox* keeps it. The user can be explicitly selected at design time or specified as an alias, which is resolved at run time. It can also be specified that the performer of the preceding activity is responsible for selecting this performer.

7. Some users from a group—a specified number of users from a group will perform this activity. All are notified, but the first users (the specified number) to acquire the task from their inboxes keep it.

The best practice for designing workflow templates is *not* to specify the performers explicitly. If the performers are explicitly identified at design time the template might not be portable across multiple repositories. It is best left for the performers to be identified at run time—the workflow initiator can pick the performers, the performer of an activity can pick the performers for the following activity, or the server can determine the performers by resolving aliases.

In the hiring process example, an alias could be used to identify the performer group for *Interview Candidate*. This would enable the same template to be used by different departments, which have different groups of people interviewing candidates.

An activity can require **electronic sign-off** from the performer for completing the activity. Electronic sign-off is performed by providing the password used for user authentication.

Activity Transitions

Workflows process objects (typically documents) through performers completing activities. These objects are carried through the workflow using **packages**. A package is identified by a *name*, *object type*, and a *version* of the object. In the hiring process example, the package called `resume` is of type `dm_document`, and uses CURRENT version.

A **flow** connects two activities in a workflow. A flow carries one or more packages from one activity to another when the first activity completes. Therefore, the first activity cannot complete unless the packages for each of its outgoing flows have been prepared. Task manager performs this validation at run time.

In the hiring process example, each flow carries the resume from one activity to another. If the resume is modified and versioned in one activity the next activity will get the new version in the package, assuming that the new version was set to be the CURRENT version. The following screenshot displays the flow properties:

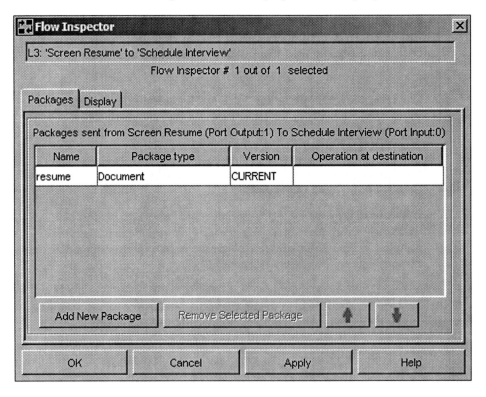

Every flow, except the ending flow, must carry one or more packages. The object type for a given package name must remain the same on all flows in a workflow template.

When an activity completes, it attempts to transition the workflow into the next activity or activities. These transitions happen along the outgoing flows from this activity. The flows can include **forward** paths and a **reject** path. Usually, the forward paths indicate normal progress and the reject path signifies an exceptional situation.

In the hiring example, most of the paths are forward and there is only one reject path—from *Schedule Interview* to *Screen Resume*. If during *Schedule Interview*, it is found that the candidate is unreachable or no longer available, the reject path can be taken and then the resume can be sent to *Discard Resume*.

There can be multiple flows going out of an activity and, therefore, it is possible to trigger multiple following activities. The flow to select after the completion of the activity can also be determined automatically through logic utilizing properties of the workflow, the task, or the package.

In order for the next activity to trigger, the following conditions can be specified as required:

1. A combination of prior tasks has completed (corresponding flows are selected) either:

   a. All of the incoming flows that are selected

   b. A specified number of the incoming flows that are selected

2. An event (system or user-defined), if specified, is sent to performer inbox programmatically.

Once the template has been defined and saved, it can be validated. If there are no errors, the state changes to validated. A validated template can be installed into the repository for use.

Use

At run time, a workflow is created from a workflow template. Activities in the workflow templates are instantiated as tasks and delivered as notifications to performers' inboxes. In Webtop, workflow reports provide information about the current states of the existing workflows.

For starting a workflow via Webtop, the user needs to have coordinator client capability. There are two basic ways of starting a workflow in Webtop:

- *Start Workflow*: Start Workflow enables selection of a workflow template first and packages can be added later.
- *Start Attachments*: Start Attachments lets you select the objects first and then a workflow template can be selected.

With either approach, the following actions need to be taken:

1. Provide a description for the workflow
2. Add comments
3. Select activity performers if needed

Another way to start a workflow is to use **quick flow**. A quick flow is an *ad hoc* workflow, which is also known as a *send to distribution list* workflow. A quick flow has one activity per performer and can be structured in one of the two ways—sequential or parallel.

If the activities are arranged sequentially, there is also a reject flow from each activity. The reject flow can go to the previous activity performer or to the initiator, but it is the same for all the activities in the quick flow (each can go to previous or each goes to the initiator). If the activities are in parallel, all the performers get their tasks simultaneously. Let's now see the interface for starting a quick flow:

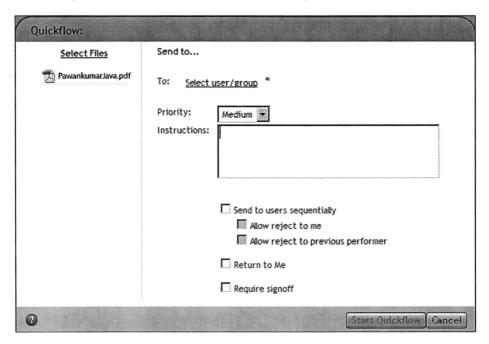

When starting a quick flow, the following information can be specified:

1. Performers
2. Structure of the quick flow—sequential or parallel
3. Instructions for completing the task
4. Whether the initiator needs to be notified for task completion
5. Whether sign-off is required
6. Priority (Low, Medium, or High)

Once a workflow starts, performers start receiving notifications in their inboxes. For example, the following figure shows a **Screen Resume** task in the performer's **Inbox**:

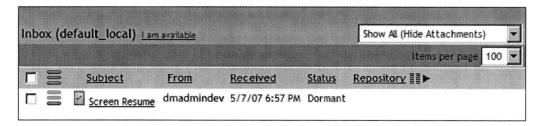

When a performer opens up a task from the inbox in Webtop, it opens the task in Task Manager. The performer can perform the desired actions and then finish the task, reject it, or forward it to someone else. The following screenshot shows the *Screen Resume* task opened in Task Manager:

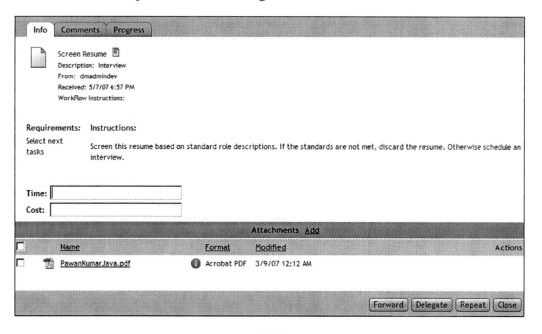

A performer can **delegate/forward** his/her task—the task is reassigned to another user or group without the intended performer completing the task. If delegation fails for any reason, the task can be sent to the workflow supervisor or to the original performer who delegated the task. This feature is useful when another user may be more suitable than the intended performer for completing the task in a special situation.

If a user is not going to be available for a period of time, this user can mark himself/herself as unavailable by identifying a **proxy**—someone who can act on this user's behalf. All tasks intended for the user are forwarded to the user's proxy automatically. When this user is available again to participate in workflows, the availability can be reset.

A performer can also request the task to be **repeated**. Repeating a task is similar to delegation, but the intended performer completes the task before reassigning to others.

The Workflow reporting can be used to monitor current and overdue tasks in various workflows. From the workflow report, a user can select a workflow and can change supervisor, or halt, resume, or terminate the workflow. The report can also be saved as a Microsoft Excel file. Recall that completed workflows can be listed for the templates with auditing enabled.

Any workflow can be selected from a workflow report for viewing its summary, which shows past and future tasks and also allows changing performers for future tasks. The audit trail entries for the workflow and progress for each task can also be viewed.

Modification

If there is a need to modify the workflow template, it needs to be uninstalled. Uninstalling a template halts the existing workflow instances for that template. The workflow template needs to be validated and installed again for the halted workflows to resume and for new workflows to be created from that template.

Documentum Product Notes

The Workflow Manager is the basic application for designing workflow templates for the Documentum platform. Once these workflow templates are validated and installed into a repository, workflow instances can be created from these templates. Tasks in the workflows are displayed to the users through clients such as Webtop and email notifications.

The Workflow Manager allows reuse of existing templates and activities in a new template. Within the Workflow Manager, existing activities or templates can be searched by cabinet or folder path, owner, name, and state. They can also be located using DQL queries. The existing templates and activities can be added to the palette and then they can be utilized for creating new templates.

Business Process Manager (BPM) is a part of the Business Process suite of products offered by EMC Documentum. BPM builds upon the core workflow capability to extend the workflows beyond the enterprise. A business process modeled through BPM can interact with email, web services, HTTP (web), FTP (file transfer), and XForms (XML forms) in tasks.

Further, activities in BPM are more configurable than in the Workflow Manager. It can also manage high volume tasks through work queues. BPM needs a DocApp to be installed in a repository before it can be used with that repository.

While BPM can be used to design business processes, Business Process Services (BPS) enable integration for incoming information over various channels. For example, BPS can receive information and content over email (SMTP), web (HTTP), or message queues (JMS) and process it in various ways, including automatic interaction with an existing workflow. Usually, BPM and BPS are used together when the process management requirements include automated integration with incoming information over the channels listed above.

Checkpoint

At this point you should be able to answer the following key questions:

1. What is a workflow? What purpose does it serve?
2. What are workflow templates, activities, performers, flows, and packages?
3. How can one execute and monitor workflow instances?

Test Your Understanding

1. A workflow template and a workflow are one and the same (True/False).
2. A workflow template is stored as an object of type:

   a. `workflow_template`

   b. `dm_wf_template`

   c. `dm_process`

   d. `dm_workflow`

3. A flow represents:

    a. Activity

    b. Package

    c. Activity transition

    d. None of the above

4. A reject flow and a forward flow going out of an activity cannot be selected simultaneously (True/False).

5. It is a good practice to use aliases in workflow templates (True/False).

6. A workflow template can be in one of the following states:

    a. Draft

    b. Validated

    c. Installed

    d. Uninstalled

7. In Webtop, a workflow can be started by:

    a. Selecting a workflow template first and then selecting documents to package

    b. Selecting documents first and then attaching to a workflow template

    c. Selecting documents without selecting a workflow template

    d. None of the above

8. Performers selected for a Quick Flow can be required to:

    a. Perform the task serially

    b. Perform the task in parallel

    c. Only one performer can be selected

    d. None of the above

9. When delegating a task, the performer must complete the task himself/herself first (True/False).

10. While a user is marked unavailable, all the tasks with this user as performer are automatically delegated to another user (True/False).

12
Lifecycles

In this chapter, we will explore the following concepts:

- Designing lifecycles
- Using lifecycles

Business Process and Content Management

Workflows enable content-centric business process automation on Documentum. Workflows carry one or more objects through various activities performed by different performers. *Lifecycles* add a powerful dimension to this mix by enabling documents to move through states according to business rules.

Thus, Documentum not only automates business processes but also automates movement of content through various phases of its life—enforcing and automating business rules through both mechanisms. Lifecycles can also be used independently but the combination of the two opens up the possibilities for satisfying complex requirements.

The simplified, but core, difference between workflows and lifecycles is that a workflow is what people do and a lifecycle is what happens to a document. Let's extend the hiring process example from *Workflows* (Chapter 11). Recall that the key document moving through the interview process is a candidate resume. For designing a lifecycle, we need to focus on what happens to the document during this process.

Initially there is a new resume, then it goes under review, and finally a decision is made and the resume becomes inactive. Thus, we can define three normal states—**New**, **UnderReview**, and **Inactive** for this lifecycle. If for any reason, the review process is suspended, an exception state **OnHold** can be used. This lifecycle is illustrated in the following figure:

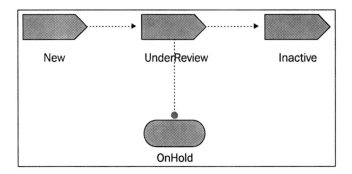

Note that these states don't have to be tied to the decision on the resume; in fact the decision can be captured in a property on the resume. The states should be designed with an eye on the progress of all the documents through this lifecycle. The states may or may not correspond directly with activities in a workflow; indeed, lifecycles can be used without involving any workflows at all.

> The differences between workflows and lifecycles are easy to highlight. A workflow is instantiated from a workflow template and actively advances one or more objects through a network of activities. A lifecycle, on the other hand, changes the states on a document in a linear fashion. There are no templates or separate instances for a lifecycle.

Lifecycle Concepts

A **lifecycle** is a set of linearly connected **states** that define the stages in an object's life. A state can be a **normal state** or an **exception state**. Normal states are used for normal progress through the stages and exception states help to deal with less frequent situations.

A lifecycle is associated with a set of object types and only objects of these types can **apply** this lifecycle. An object can be associated with at most one lifecycle at a time and it is in exactly one of the states present in the lifecycle. The object can move back and forth between the lifecycle states following the specified conditions and triggering changes in the process.

A state can have **entry criteria** that must be satisfied for an object to enter that state. When an object is about to enter a state, **entry actions** specified for that state are executed. Once an object has entered a state, any specified **post-entry (post-change) actions** are executed. Actions can be predefined actions or custom ones.

These concepts are discussed in detail in the rest of the chapter.

Lifecycles and Customization

Just like workflows, lifecycles are also a key component of Documentum customization. Lifecycles are usually bundled with other customization components in DocApps (see the chapter on DocApps for details).

A document lifecycle can be developed in the following manner:

1. *Analyze*: The information is gathered about the relevant document types (or object types, in general) and the stages a document will need to go through. Also consider the conditions for state changes and what actions may be associated with them.

2. *Model*: The lifecycle is modeled in terms of states, entry criteria, entry actions, and post-entry actions.

3. *Define*: The model is formalized as a lifecycle using DAB. The lifecycle is validated and installed into the desired repository.

4. *Use*: Business users with appropriate access start applying the lifecycle to objects. The objects can progress through the states via workflows, manual actions, or scheduled actions.

5. *Modify*: If the lifecycle needs to be modified, it is uninstalled, modified, validated, and installed again.

The following sections describe the above-mentioned steps in more detail.

Analysis

Analysis of business rules for defining document lifecycles involves gathering information regarding the important stages in the life of a document type and the details around the transitions between these stages. Some additional information may also be captured about how the documents need to be managed within Documentum, as they progress through these stages. For example, it may be desirable to move the document to a new location and restrict access after a certain point in the document's lifecycle.

In the hiring process example, analysis may require talking to the Human Resources managers and the interviewers to understand if they want to sort resumes in different folders as they move through the hiring process and are later archived.

Modeling and Definition

Modeling and definition of lifecycles share several aspects and are discussed together in this section to avoid repetition. Modeling maps the requirements for the lifecycles to Documentum terminology to facilitate definition. The model is defined in a Documentum repository as a lifecycle using the Lifecycle Editor in Documentum Application Builder (DAB).

A **lifecycle** is a set of linearly connected states that define the stages in an object's life. A lifecycle is usually designed using DAB and is stored in the repository as dm_policy object. During development, the lifecycle has *draft* status. It can be validated for any errors and its status changes to *validated* if there are no errors. It is also possible to provide custom Docbasic procedures or SBOs (Service-based Business Objects) for performing custom validation. SBOs were discussed in *Architecture* (Chapter 4).

A validated lifecycle can be installed into a repository to make it available to all users, whereby its status changes to *installed*. However, a lifecycle is associated with a type and possible subtypes and this lifecycle can only be applied to the objects of these types. Let's now see the DAB screen for creating and editing a lifecycle:

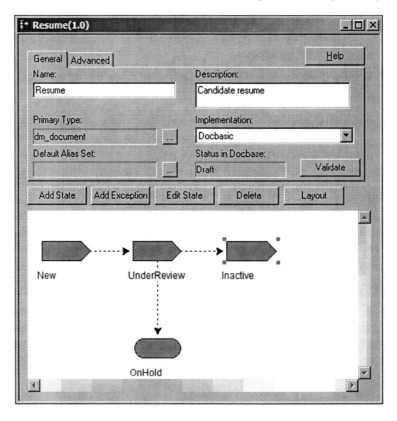

Validation of a lifecycle checks the minimum requirements on the following:

- *Security*: The security requirement mandates that the user has *write* permission on the lifecycle.
- *Consistency*: The consistency requirements mandate that the acceptable types are subtypes of the primary type and the properties, procedures, etc. referred to in the lifecycle actually exist.
- *Validity*: The remaining validity requirements are that the current status of the lifecycle is *draft*, the lifecycle has at least one attachable state, and the primary type is dm_sysobject or one of its subtypes other than dm_policy.

 dm_sysobject and all its subtypes except dm_policy can be selected to be associated with a lifecycle.

Just like workflows, aliases can be used to make lifecycles portable across multiple repositories and business situations. A default alias set can be specified for a lifecycle and the aliases are resolved at run time. The alias resolution for objects with lifecycles is discussed in Chapter 13.

States

A **state** in a lifecycle represents a stage in the life of an object. There are two types of states:

- **Normal**: Each lifecycle has normal states, which include a *start* or *base* state, some intermediate *step* states, and a final *end* state. Each state can define behavior such as change of location, permissions, and ownership for the object. This capability facilitates automated management of content as it moves through the lifecycle.

  The following figure shows a portion of the resume lifecycle described earlier, where the **UnderReview** state is a normal state:

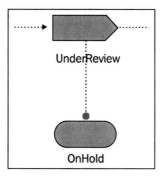

- **Exceptional**: Optionally, a lifecycle can also have **exception states** to represent unusual situations. One lifecycle can have multiple exception states but there can be no more than one exception state per normal state.

  However, several normal states can use the same exception state. A lifecycle can be **suspended** by moving from a normal state to an exception state and this suspension can be temporary or permanent. At that point, it can only be **resumed** to the same normal state or back to the base state. In the figure on the previous page, **OnHold** is an exception state associated with **UnderReview**. For example, the OnHold state could be used to handle the situation where the candidate may be sick and unavailable for interview.

The following screenshot shows the DAB screen for editing a state:

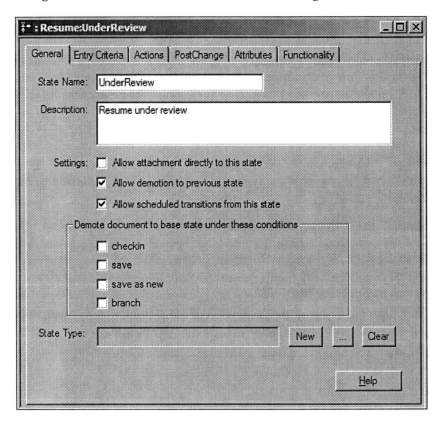

It is also possible to *schedule* an automatic state transition at a predefined date and time. This feature can be used to prevent objects from getting stuck in a state indefinitely. This feature is implemented via a job that moves objects out of the specific state at a given date and time.

A state can define how object attributes (properties) behave while an object is in this state. An attribute may get a new value in this state. The label and help may be changed for the attribute. The state can also specify whether the attribute will become read-only, nullable, or hidden while the object is in this state. An attribute can be made modifiable while the overall object is immutable when it is in this state.

Note that, unlike for workflows, there is no concept of a template and instances for lifecycles. Information related to the lifecycle state of an object is captured in the object itself. The following object properties, inherited from dm_sysobject, capture this information:

1. dm_sysobject.r_policy_id identifies the lifecycle applied to the object. This is shown in the following figure:

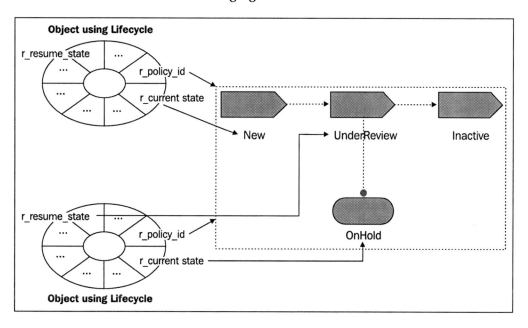

2. dm_sysobject.r_current_state identifies the current state of the object in the associated lifecycle.

3. dm_sysobject.r_resume_state identifies the normal state to resume to, if the current state is an exception state.

An object can be attached to a lifecycle and be processed by a workflow at the same time. In fact, this combination provides great flexibility in terms of implementing and enforcing business rules.

Recall that an object is processed by a workflow in the form of a package component. A package can have multiple components and `dmi_package.r_component_id` stores the object IDs of its components.

State Transitions

The sole purpose of a lifecycle is to move objects through the states in the lifecycle and everything of interest happens during or right after a state transition.

When an object changes state from a normal state to another normal state it is called **promotion** or **demotion**. Promotion moves an object from one normal state to the *next* normal state within its lifecycle. Demotion can move the object from one normal state to the *previous* normal state or to the base state.

Conditions may be configured on a state that specify when demoting from this state leads to the base state rather than to the previous state. It should be obvious that promotion is not possible from the final state and demotion is not possible from the base state.

When an object changes state between a normal state and an exception state it is called **suspension** or **resumption**. An object can be suspended from a normal state to the associated exception state. From an exception state, the object can be resumed to the state from where it was suspended.

When a transition from state A to state B is triggered the following sequence of steps is executed:

1. Evaluate entry criteria for state B. If true, perform step 2.
2. Perform entry actions for state B. If they complete successfully perform step 3.
3. Change state to B.
4. Perform post-entry actions for state B.

The following flowchart shows the steps in a better way:

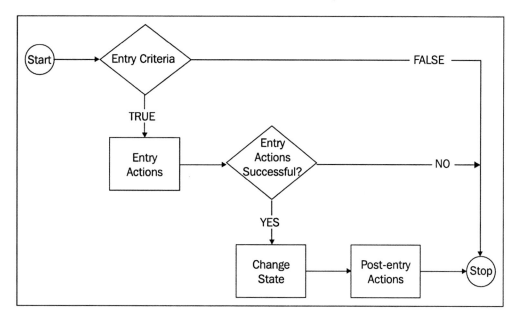

Now, let's see the steps in more detail.

Entry criteria for a state are the conditions that must be met before promote, suspend, or resume operations can move an object to this state. Entry criteria are also checked when a lifecycle is attached to an object, since the object enters the initial state at this point. The criteria can be specified as Boolean expressions on object properties or as Java or Docbasic procedures. For one lifecycle either all entry criteria procedures are Java or all are Docbasic; they cannot be mixed.

 A demote operation does not check for entry criteria. Also entry criteria are bypassed for the lifecycle owner and superuser and are not enforced by the Content Server in these cases.

Entry actions are performed if the entry criteria evaluate to *true*. If the entry actions complete successfully, the object enters the new state. Entry actions can be standard system-defined or custom user-defined ones. At run time, system-defined actions are performed prior to user-defined actions.

The standard system-defined actions include the following:

1. Set Attribute: Set a value for a specified property

2. Add to Repeating Attribute: Add a value to a repeating property

3. Remove from Repeating Attribute: Remove a value from a repeating property

4. Add Version Label: Add a version label

5. Remove Version Label: Remove a version label

6. Set Owner: Set owner name (change owner)

7. Set Permission Set: Assign a permission set (change permission)

8. Link to New Location: Link the object to another folder/cabinet using a folder path or a location alias. The `$value()` keyword can be used to utilize property values in specifying location. `$value()` was discussed in *Custom Types* (Chapter 9).

9. Remove Link from Existing Location: Remove a link to the object from a folder/cabinet

10. Move All Links to Location: Move all the links to the object to another folder/cabinet

11. Request Rendition: Request a rendition of the object

The user-defined actions can be Docbasic procedures or Java methods.

Post-entry actions are performed right after entering the new state. For example, if the object represents web content and the state is Active a post-entry action may publish the content automatically. Another example of a post-entry action is to start a workflow on the object. Post-entry actions can also be implemented in Java or Docbasic.

The security configuration for lifecycle action (entry action and post-entry action) execution can be set up globally for a repository in `dm_docbase_config.a_ bpaction_run_as`. This property can be set to one of the following values:

1. `session_user`: Current user (default value)

2. `superuser`: Superuser

3. `lifecycle_owner`: Lifecycle owner

4. Specific username

The user for running the lifecycle actions must have the appropriate permissions for performing those actions. For example, if an action changes the location of the object the user must have *Change Location* extended permission.

Use

Once a lifecycle has been installed into the repository, it can be used with the objects of types supported by the lifecycle. A lifecycle can be applied to an object of one of the associated types and then the object progresses through the lifecycle states according to the configured rules.

When a lifecycle is applied to an object, the object enters the initial state. An object can only be associated with one lifecycle at a time. Since different versions of an object are two separate objects, they can be attached to different lifecycles.

> A **default lifecycle** can be specified for a custom type. When an object is created for this custom type, the default lifecycle can be applied to it without explicitly selecting the specific lifecycle. This capability removes the need for the end users to identify a specific lifecycle.

In order to apply a lifecycle to an object, the user must have *relate* permission on the lifecycle or be the object owner.

An object can change state manually or automatically. For example, a workflow activity can result in a change of state. Changing the state of an object requires *Write* permission and *Change State* extended permission on the object.

In Webtop, the lifecycle ID and state for an object can be viewed on the property sheet.

Modification

It is possible to modify a lifecycle after it has been installed and applied to objects. If the lifecycle needs to be edited, it is uninstalled and objects using this lifecycle cannot change their states. Once the modifications are completed, the lifecycle should be checked in, validated, and installed again.

> It is recommended not to create multiple versions of one lifecycle. The lifecycle should be checked in as the same version.

Help—Some DQL Queries

While DAB and Webtop can be used to interact with objects and lifecycles, the following queries can be used to obtain specific information directly.

The following DQL query identifies the lifecycle ID, current state, and the resume state (meaningful only if the current state is an exception state) for a document. Note, however, that all of this information is system data (internal) and not user-friendly. This information neither names the policy nor the states; they are all numbers.

```
SELECT r_policy_id, r_current_state, r_resume_state
FROM dm_document
WHERE object_name like 'MyDocument%'
```

The user-friendly information can be obtained from the lifecycle separately or by joining with the above query. The following query lists information about the states in a lifecycle named *Resume*:

```
SELECT object_name, state_name, state_description, state_class
FROM dm_policy
WHERE object_name = 'Resume'
```

Note that the state properties queried above are repeating properties and list all the states. Information about a particular state cannot be extracted using an index, such as state_name[0], in a DQL query. All the repeating values are retrieved when a repeating attribute is selected. However, DFC can retrieve values at specific indices.

Another helpful query can display the status of each lifecycle. For lifecycle status, r_definition_state value equal to 0 means draft, 1 means validated, and 2 means installed.

```
SELECT object_name, r_definition_state
FROM dm_policy
```

Documentum Product Notes

Lifecycles are designed using the lifecycle editor in Documentum Application Builder. Typically, lifecycles are bundled in DocApps along with workflows and other customizations. Lifecycles provide powerful automation capabilities that can be used independently of workflows.

Checkpoint

At this point you should be able to answer the following key questions:

1. What is a lifecycle? What purpose does it serve? How is it different from a workflow?

2. What are states, state transitions, entry criteria, entry actions, post-entry actions?

3. How can one apply lifecycles and check object states?

Test Your Understanding

1. A lifecycle cannot be used without a workflow (True/False).

2. In order to use a lifecycle:

    a. It must be instantiated

    b. It must be installed

    c. It must be applied to an object

    d. None of the above

3. The entry criteria are evaluated on every state change (True/False).

4. If a valid lifecycle has a Java-based entry action, the following can be added to the lifecycle while still keeping it valid:

    a. Another Java-based entry action

    b. A Java-based post-entry action

    c. A Docbasic-based entry action

    d. A Docbasic-based post-entry action

5. For applying a lifecycle, the user must know its name (True/False).

6. It is not sufficient for entry criteria to pass for a state change to succeed (True/False).

7. A lifecycle is stored as an object of type:

    a. `dm_lifecycle`

    b. `dmi_lifecycle`

    c. `dm_policy`

    d. `dmi_policy`

8. The lifecycle state of an object is stored in:
   a. Properties of the object
   b. Properties of the lifecycle
   c. Properties of the lifecycle instance
   d. None of the above

9. One normal state can be associated with:
   a. One exception state
   b. One exception state but that exception state cannot be associated with another normal state
   c. More than one exception state
   d. None of the above

10. A lifecycle action can be run as:
    a. Superuser
    b. Lifecycle owner
    c. Current user
    d. A specific user

Part 5

Advanced Concepts

Aliases

Virtual Documents

13
Aliases

In this chapter, we will explore the following concepts:

- Creating aliases and alias sets
- Referencing aliases
- Alias resolution

Customization—Reusability and Portability

Documentum customization involves multiple aspects at various architecture layers and these customizations can easily become fairly complex. This complexity can be compounded by the fact that developing and deploying customizations often involves multiple environments—development, QA, and production are typical. Further, multiple departments in an enterprise may have separate repositories of their own.

For example if there are two departments and three environments for each department, it leads to a total of six repositories if a clean separation is maintained. Ideally, customization developed in one repository should be easily ported to all these repositories. This portability is achieved by parameterizing everything that can be different across these repositories such that the parameters specific to a repository can be specified/evaluated when the customization is deployed to a repository.

The customization artefacts are bundled together in DocApps and making customizations portable effectively means making DocApps and their contents portable. Documentum supports the use of **aliases**, which act as placeholders for values that can be inserted at an appropriate time before they are needed. Thus, aliases can be used to handle the differences among repositories and they get replaced with values specific to the repository when they are deployed and used within a specific repository.

For example, the following figure shows a DocApp that references the aliases named `interviewer` and `dept_vp`. These aliases could be used for providing appropriate permissions to these users. However, each repository is responsible for providing the values for these aliases such that they can be dynamically determined. The real users are different in different repositories but they get similar rights if they replace the same alias reference.

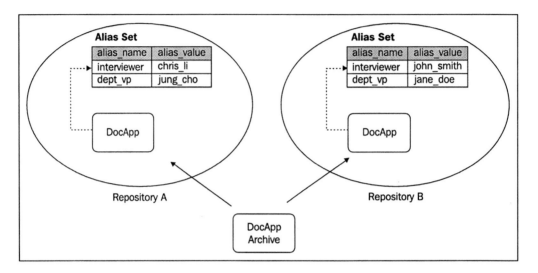

An alias can represent a user, a group, a location (folder path within a repository), or a permission set—these are the typical aspects that vary across repositories. An **alias set** bundles several aliases and, optionally, their values together to form a key mechanism for making customizations reusable and portable. In addition to the portability benefits across repositories, aliases provide similar benefits within a repository in situations where parameterizing is helpful.

 A simplistic, but fundamentally sound, view of alias sets is that of a lookup table containing key-value pairs. Each row in the table corresponds to an alias.

Aliases

An **alias** is a placeholder name, which needs to be replaced with a value before it can be used. For example, suppose an interviewer needs to be granted certain permissions on a candidate resume, but interviewers can be different for different candidates. In this case, an alias can be created for the interviewer that can be replaced with a real user when the permissions are to be granted to the interviewer.

In a way, an alias acts like a variable in a program that can be specified by a name but whose value is used when the program is run. This allows the developer to create only one permission set and many alias sets rather than many permission sets. Managing a permission set is more complex than managing an alias set. Further, many similar permission sets may become a nightmare to manage when changes may be required for all of them.

In general, an alias can represent a user, a group, a folder location (path in a repository), or a permission set. However, when an alias is stored its type identifies the specific intent for each alias in terms of an **alias type**:

- Unknown (0)
- User (1)
- Group (2)
- User or Group (3)
- Cabinet path (4)
- Folder path (5)
- ACL name (6)

In most cases, the Content Server is responsible for recognizing that a property actually contains a reference to an alias and for resolving it (replacing the placeholder with a desired value) at an appropriate time. There are only certain properties of certain types that the Content Server examines for the presence of an alias. These properties are as listed:

Property	Type	Description
owner_name	dm_sysobject	Owner of an object
acl_domain	dm_sysobject	Owner of the permission set associated with an object
acl_name	dm_sysobject	Name of the permission associated with an object
r_accessor_name	dm_acl	User or group getting permission in this permission set template
performer_name	dm_activity	Performer of a workflow activity

There is one other place where aliases are recognized — in the `folderSpec` argument of the `link` and `unlink` DFC methods. This argument specifies the folder path (or folder object ID) where an object is linked or unlinked. The signatures for these methods for sysobjects are as shown:

```
public void link   (String folderSpec) throws DfException
public void unlink (String folderSpec) throws DfException
```

Note that custom attributes are not examined by the Content Server for the presence of aliases. However, applications (custom code) can examine custom attributes and provide a resolution mechanism.

Alias Sets

Aliases are stored as sets called **alias sets**. An alias set is stored as an object of type `dm_alias_set`. The information about each alias is stored in three repeating properties of an alias set, which correspond to each other via identical indices.

Property	Description
alias_name	Name of an alias
alias_value	Value for the alias, may or may not be present
alias_category	Type of alias, various types described earlier

Managing Alias Sets

Alias sets can be created in Documentum Application Builder (DAB), Documentum Administrator (DA), DQL/API queries, or custom DFC applications. The following figure shows an alias set in DA:

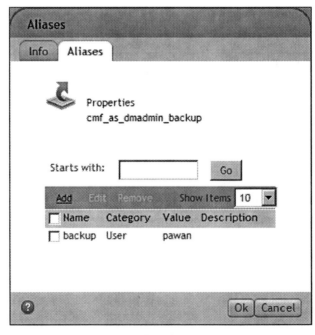

Let's now see the same alias set in DAB:

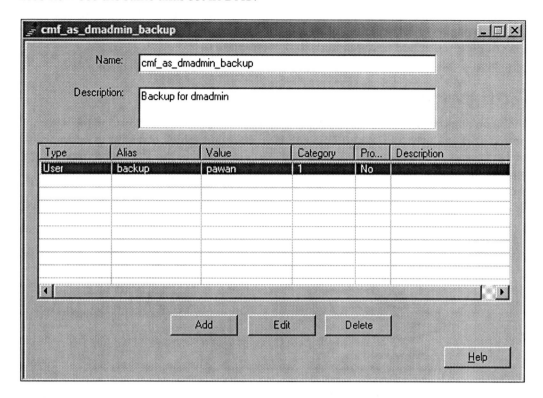

While alias sets can be created and stored unrelated to other objects, they are typically useful only after being associated with one of the following:

Object Type	Property	Description
dm_workflow	r_alias_set_id	Object ID of the alias set used to resolve performer aliases when the workflow is created. It is a run-time copy of the alias set identified in perf_alias_set_id of the dm_process (workflow template) object.
Session config (non-persistent)	alias_set	Session-level default alias set.
dm_user	alias_set_id	User-level default alias set.
dm_group	alias_set_id	Group-level default alias set.
dm_server_config	alias_set_id	System-level (Content Server level) default alias set.
dm_policy	alias_set_ids	Alias sets for a lifecycle.

One alias name can appear in multiple alias sets and in certain scenarios it may be desirable as well. There is a mechanism called alias resolution, which is used by the Content Server for selecting alias sets for looking up the value of an alias. Alias resolution is described in detail later in this chapter.

Referencing Aliases

When an alias needs to be used as a placeholder its **reference** is stored using a `%` prefix. This is a way to distinguish an alias from other values. An alias is referenced as `%alias_set_name.alias_name` or `%alias_name`. When the alias set name is omitted from a reference, the alias name is searched for in one or more alias sets according to the alias resolution rules, which are described later. The following figure shows how an alias named `interviewer` is referenced in another object:

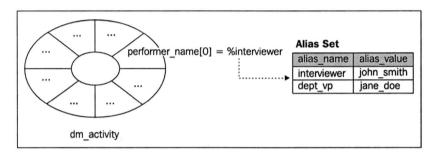

A **permission set template** (also known as **ACL template**) is a special type of object that uses aliases. A permission set that contains one or more alias references to users or groups in the `r_accessor_name` property is known as permission set template. The type of a permission set is identified by the `dm_acl.acl_class` property, which can have one of the following values:

Permission Set Type	Description
0	Private permission set
1	Permission set template
2	Instance of permission set template
3	Public permission set

Permission sets are discussed in detail in *Object Security* (Chapter 7).

Permission set templates can be created in DAB only; Webtop or DA user interfaces do not support creation of permission set templates currently, as of Documentum 5.3 SP4 release.

Resolving Aliases

Aliases provide placeholders for users, groups, locations, and permission sets. When a real value is substituted for a placeholder (alias reference), the alias is said to be **resolved**. Thus, **alias resolution** completes the missing information such that the objects and properties dependent on the aliases become available for use.

Alias resolution looks up the appropriate value for an alias name from an alias set. If the alias set name is present in the reference, the process of lookup is straightforward — pick up the value corresponding to the alias name from the specified alias set.

On the other hand, if the alias set name is omitted the Content Server tries to locate an appropriate alias set to look up the alias value. This lookup process utilizes a concept referred to as the **scope** of alias sets.

An alias scope is the visibility of an alias set for resolving aliases in various situations, including the object using the alias, the context, and the values of other properties. If the alias set name is present in a reference, the alias scope is the alias set name. When the reference does not include an alias set name, a sequence of alias sets is searched. This sequence of alias sets (scopes) is different for different objects and contexts. The following figure shows how an alias is resolved after checking three alias sets for the presence of an alias named `interviewer`:

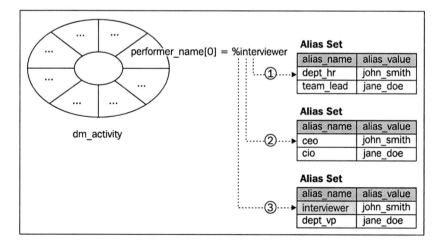

The Content Server follows different approaches for alias resolution in the following situations:

1. A workflow activity needs to be started and its performer refers to an alias
2. A sysobject is saved
3. The DFC link or unlink method is invoked
4. A permission set template is assigned to an object

The alias resolution approaches for these situations are described in detail now.

Workflow Alias Resolution

A workflow activity (`dm_activity`) may contain an alias reference without an alias set name in the `performer_name` property. This alias is resolved when the activity is started in a workflow instance. The sequence of alias scopes searched for this purpose is dependent on the value of `resolve_type` property of the activity. The value of `resolve_type` can be normal resolution path (0), alias set associated with incoming package (1), or alias set associated with user or group (2). Let's now look at the resolution sequence for each of these situations.

Default Sequence

When `dm_activity.resolve_type = 0` is true for an activity, the following sequence of alias scopes is searched to resolve any alias reference in `performer_name`:

1. The alias set specified on the workflow instance—`dm_workflow.r_alias_set_id`. The workflow instance gets a copy of the alias set specified in the corresponding workflow template (`dm_process.perf_alias_set_id`).
2. The alias set present in the session, i.e. non-persistent session config object—`alias_set`.
3. The alias set of the performer of the previous activity – `dm_user.alias_set_id`.
4. The alias set of the default group of the performer of the previous activity—`dm_group.alias_set_id`.
5. The alias set of the server configuration—`dm_server_config.alias_set_id`.

Package Sequence

When `dm_activity.resolve_type = 1` is true for an activity, the following sequence of alias scopes is searched to resolve any alias reference in `performer_name`. The alias set of a package component is used—`dm_sysobject.r_alias_set_id`. The components are examined in the order they are stored within the package. Packages are discussed in *Workflows* (Chapter 11).

There can be multiple package components, so there is an additional step of first identifying the appropriate package. If `dm_activity.resolve_pkg_name` is present, the components of this package are searched. Otherwise, packages are examined in the order of their storage as described earlier.

User Sequence

When `dm_activity.resolve_type = 2` is true for an activity, the following sequence of alias scopes is searched to resolve any alias reference in `performer_name`:

1. The alias set of the performer of the previous activity—`dm_user.alias_set_id`.
2. The alias set of the default group of the performer of the previous activity—`dm_group.alias_set_id`.

Resolution Process

The resolution process for aliases in workflows consists of two key steps—the referenced alias is located using scopes as described earlier and then the resolved alias is validated to be of a suitable type.

The validation is carried out by matching `dm_activity.performer_type` against the `alias_category` on the selected alias set. The performer type can be any of the following:

- Workflow supervisor (0)
- Repository owner (1)
- Last performer (2)
- User (3)
- All members in a group (4)
- Any user in a group (5)
- The member who has the least number of tasks (6)
- Some members of a group, or some users in the repository (8)
- Some members of a group, or some users in the repository *sequentially* (9)
- A user from a work queue (10)

Valid alias types (`alias_category`) are user (1), group (2), and user or group (3).

 Note that there is no valid performer type with value 7 in version 5.3.

It is possible for the resolution process to be unsuccessful; no suitable substitution is found for the placeholder alias reference. This can happen in three cases:

1. The referenced alias name is not found in any of the scopes.
2. The alias name is found but there is no corresponding value.
3. The alias name is found but the alias type is not compatible with the performer type on the activity.

When the alias resolution fails for any reason, a warning is generated and the workflow supervisor is notified. The task corresponding to the activity is also assigned to the supervisor.

Sysobject Alias Resolution

When a sysobject is saved, the following sequence of scopes is examined:

1. Alias set of the sysobject—`dm_sysobject.r_alias_set_id`.
2. Alias set present in the session (`alias_set`).
3. Alias set of the current user—`dm_user.alias_set_id`.
4. Alias set of the default group of the current user—`dm_group.alias_set_id`.
5. Alias set of the server configuration—`dm_server_config.alias_set_id`.

 The same sequences are also examined for the alias resolution for the `folderSpec` argument of DFC `link` and `unlink` methods.

Permission Set Template Alias Resolution

When a permission set template (ACL template) is assigned to an object, a copy of the permission set template is created, the alias references in the accessor names are resolved, and references are replaced with actual values. Finally, this copy of the permission set is assigned as a custom permission set to the object. The sequence of alias sets examined in the resolution process depends on whether a lifecycle has been applied to the object. Let's now have a look at the two cases.

Object with Lifecycle

When an object is associated with a lifecycle, its alias set has possibly been assigned by the lifecycle. Therefore, the alias resolution does not look at any alias set other than that currently assigned to the object. The alias set of the sysobject is `dm_sysobject.r_alias_set_id`.

Object without Lifecycle

When a permission set template is assigned to an object without a lifecycle, the following sequence of alias sets is examined:

1. Alias set present in the session — `alias_set`.
2. Alias set of the current user — `dm_user.alias_set_id`.
3. Alias set of the default group of the current user — `dm_group.alias_set_id`.
4. Alias set of the server configuration — `dm_server_config.alias_set_id`.

[The search for alias value stops with an error if the alias name is found, but no value is present in that alias set.]

Lifecycle Alias Set Resolution

When a lifecycle with multiple alias sets is applied to an object, it needs to be determined which *alias set* should be applied to the object. Note that this process is not resolving an alias, rather it is identifying an alias set to apply, which can later be used for alias resolution. As a result of the following process, `dm_sysobject.r_alias_set` will be set if an appropriate alias set is found:

1. Check if `alias_set` in session config is present in `dm_policy.alias_set_ids` for the lifecycle. If found use this, otherwise continue.

2. Check if `dm_user.alias_set_id` for the current user is present in `dm_policy.alias_set_ids` for the lifecycle. If found use this, otherwise continue.

3. Check if `dm_group.alias_set_id` of the default group for the current user is present in `dm_policy.alias_set_ids` for the lifecycle. If found use this, otherwise continue.

4. Check if `dm_server_config.alias_set_id` for the server configuration is present in `dm_policy.alias_set_ids` for the lifecycle. If found use this, otherwise continue.

5. Use the alias set specified by `dm_policy.alias_set_ids[0]`, also known as the default alias set of the lifecycle.

Help—Some DQL Queries

Some helpful queries related to alias sets are described here. These queries are based on the information provided in this chapter.

The following query retrieves aliases (names, values, and types) present in an alias set:

```
SELECT alias_name, alias_value, alias_category
FROM dm_alias_set
WHERE object_name = 'my_alias_set'
```

The following query retrieves the performer names for an activity:

```
SELECT performer_name
FROM dm_activity
WHERE object_name = 'Screen Resume'
```

The following query retrieves the accessor names for permission set templates:

```
SELECT r_object_id, object_name, r_accessor_name
FROM dm_acl
WHERE acl_class=1
```

Documentum Product Notes

Alias sets can be created in DAB, DA, DQL/API, or a custom DFC application. The Content Server resolves alias references in certain properties of certain types of objects and in the folderSpec argument of link and unlink DFC methods. The custom properties can contain alias references but the Content Server does not resolve them.

ACL templates can only be created in DAB.

Checkpoint

At this point you should be able to answer the following key questions:

1. What are aliases and alias sets? What purpose do they serve?

2. How are alias references used and resolved in various scenarios?

Test Your Understanding

1. An alias set and a permission set are one and the same thing (True/False).

2. A regular permission set does not contain any alias references (True/False).

3. An alias can contain a value of the following type:

    a. User

    b. Folder path in repository

    c. Folder path on the client

    d. Permission set name

4. The Content Server resolves aliases for the following properties:

    a. `dm_acl.performer_name`

    b. `dm_activity.r_accessor_name`

    c. `dm_sysobject.acl_domain`

    d. `dm_sysobject.acl_name`

5. It is possible to link an object to a folder, without explicitly identifying the folder by its path or object ID (True/False).

6. The following are valid alias references:

    a. `%purchasing.manager%`

    b. `%purchasing%.manager`

    c. `%purchasing.manager`

    d. `%manager`

7. If a permission set template is applied to four different objects, how many new custom permission sets are created?

    a. 0

    b. 3

    c. 4

    d. 5

8. When aliases are resolved for an object with a lifecycle, how many alias sets may be examined?

    a. 0

    b. 1

    c. 3

    d. 4

9. Alias resolution for a workflow activity can fail in the following ways:

    a. Alias name is not found

    b. Alias value is not found

    c. Alias value is not compatible with performer type

    d. None of the above

10. The algorithm for alias resolution uses the concept of:

    a. Locality

    b. Persistence

    c. Scope

    d. None of the above

14
Virtual Documents

In this chapter, we will explore the following concepts:

- Managing virtual documents
- Using virtual documents

Managing Content Hierarchically

The hierarchical content is fairly common in everyday life. A book is an excellent example of hierarchical content. Books are usually organized into chapters, chapters into sections, sections into sub-sections, and there can be more layers in such a hierarchy. A hierarchical organization is frequently used with large content to *facilitate* its management. While this benefit applies even to content that is not in electronic form, significant benefits are possible for electronic content. This is what the hierarchy for a book looks like:

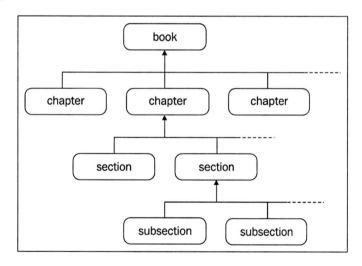

While the hierarchical organization makes large content manageable, it also opens up new possibilities for *online collaboration*. For example, suppose a team working on creation of a book consists of two authors, two subject matter reviewers, and one editor. It is highly desirable that all these participants be able to work on various portions (sometimes even the same portions) of the book in order to complete their tasks efficiently and effectively.

Documentum enables hierarchical content management through **virtual documents**. Virtual documents allow parts of a document to be treated as independent documents. From another perspective, a set of independent documents can be combined and treated as one document.

Virtual documents offer various benefits. One document can be *reused* in multiple virtual documents. While this may not be readily applicable to books (content is rarely repeated in an identical form across multiple books), it is fairly common in internal enterprise documents or product documentation. For example, the administration guide and the user guide for a product may share some common sections, which can be managed independently and reused in these two guides.

Collaboration is another great capability where multiple people can own various components of a virtual document. This capability enables each contributor to create and update the individually owned content while allowing a reviewer to look at the combined document as a whole. Virtual documents also help to overcome some technical challenges in electronic form. Usually one document has one format — doc for MS Word, pdf for Adobe Acrobat, ppt for Microsoft PowerPoint, etc. A virtual document allows documents in various formats to be combined into one virtual document.

A virtual document with various component documents evolving somewhat independently can become unwieldy. This is particularly true if the overall document needs to continue to evolve while it is also published for the general public periodically. For example, a corporate policy document may keep changing over time while approved versions get published for general use.

Documentum supports taking **snapshots** of virtual documents to deal with such challenges. A snapshot is a record of a virtual document at a specific point in time and exists separately from the virtual document itself. Snapshots enable retrieval of the exact form of the virtual document at various points in time. For the example of a book, the different editions of the book can be maintained as snapshots.

Virtual Documents

A **virtual document** is a container for **component** documents, which are either simple documents of type dm_sysobject (or a subtype excluding dm_folder and its subtypes) or virtual documents. Even though its primary purpose is to act as a container, a virtual document object can have content of its own.

 Note that it is a *recursive* definition — the definition of virtual document, in turn, uses the term virtual document. In computer science, recursive definitions facilitate description of tree-like structures. We will see in a moment that virtual documents also have a tree structure.

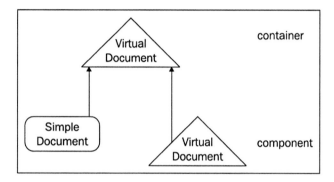

Note that there is no limit on the *depth* of the hierarchy — a virtual document can contain another virtual document, which can contain another virtual document, and so on. The containment relationship between a virtual document and its component is known as **nesting**.

The components in the virtual document hierarchy are **ordered**, which means that there is a sequence among the direct components of one virtual document that, in turn, leads to a sequence among all the components in the complete hierarchy.

Consider the book example again. The top level is just the book and the level below is chapters, which are ordered as 1, 2, 3, etc. The level below chapters consists of sections, which may be ordered as 2.1, 2.2, 2.3, etc. for Chapter 2 and similarly for others. There can also be subsections such as 2.2.1, 2.2.2, etc.

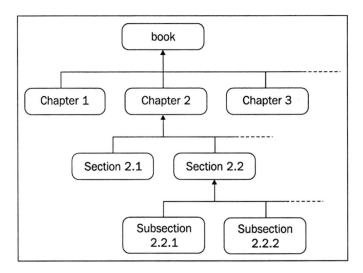

A virtual document and its components have a *parent-child relationship*. One virtual document can have many children. At the same time, one document can be a component of multiple virtual documents – this is how a document is reused in multiple virtual documents. For each document that is a component of a virtual document, the membership information (link) is stored in an object of type `dmr_containment`.

Managing Virtual Documents

Virtual documents can be managed using Webtop. Webtop supports virtual document operations through menu items, the browser-tree component, and the Virtual Document Manager component. Some of the menu options related to virtual documents are shown in the next screenshot:

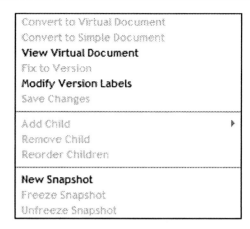

Creating Virtual Documents

A virtual document is created by converting a simple document to a virtual document. A virtual document is identified by the `dm_sysobject.r_is_virtual_doc` property being set to `1`.

Exploring a Virtual Document Structure

A virtual document is also shown at the folder level in the browser tree within Webtop. This enables browsing of the virtual document components in a way similar to exploring folder contents. Opening a virtual document in Webtop opens it in the Virtual Document Manager component. Let's now see a virtual document open in the **Virtual Document Manager** interface:

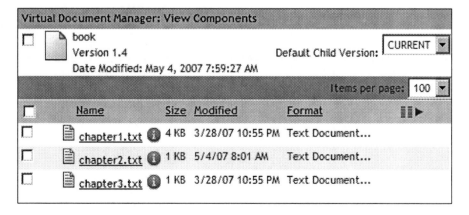

Modifying Virtual Documents

A virtual document can be modified in the following key ways:

1. Add a new component
2. Remove an existing component
3. Reorder existing components

 In Webtop, when a virtual document is modified via these operations on the components, the parent virtual document is automatically checked out.

A document can be added to a virtual document in three ways.

1. An existing document can be added to the *clipboard* and then added as a component to a virtual document. The clipboard holds files for moving, copying or linking to another location in the repository. It can hold multiple files at once.
2. A virtual document can be chosen and components added to it using the *file selector* interface. The file-selector interface enables users to browse the repository and select multiple objects from different locations.
3. A *new document* can be created and added as a component of a virtual document in one interaction.

Let's see how the file selector enables users to add multiple components to a virtual document:

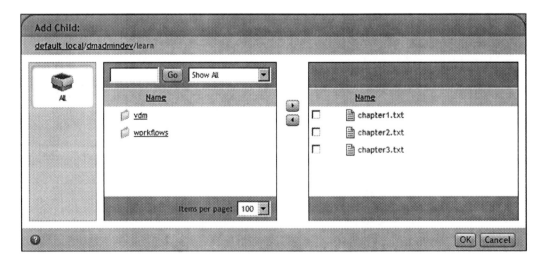

A component of a virtual document can be selected and removed.

The components of a virtual document can be **reordered** in Webtop in two ways — using *drag and drop* or using a *reorder interface*. With drag and drop the *reposition* option moves a component to its new position. The *add* option creates a copy of the dragged component in the new position. Using the reorder menu option provides an interface to move components up or down in the order.

This screenshot shows reordering of virtual document components in Webtop:

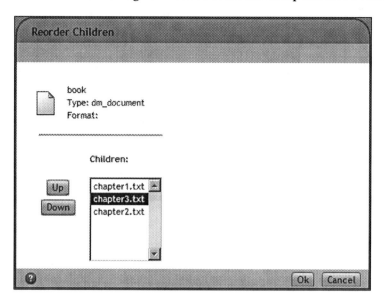

Virtual Documents—Versions

Each component of a virtual document can be independently managed and versioned. While this feature provides flexibility, it also leads to some challenges with regard to dealing with versions of the virtual document as a whole. Fortunately, Documentum provides additional capabilities to deal with such requirements.

Version labels can be managed for a virtual document in one of two ways — only for the (root) virtual document object or for the entire virtual document including its components and all indirect descendants. Thus, a version label can be added to or removed from the entire virtual document tree in the usual manner.

Since each component of a virtual document can be versioned independently, there are multiple ways for a virtual document to pick the versions of its components. It is possible to specify a **binding rule** for a component that specifies a particular version of the document to be bound to a containing virtual document.

In the Virtual Document Manager, the menu option **Fix to Version** can be used to specify a binding rule as shown:

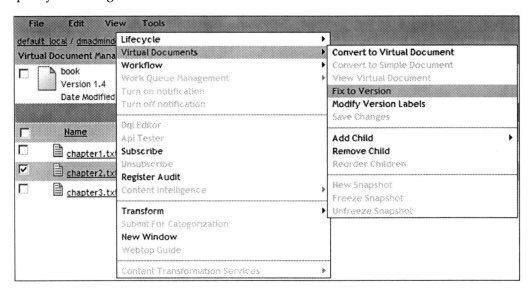

Using the **Fix to Version** option, the following alternatives are available for the binding rule:

1. Use the CURRENT version of the component document.
2. Use a specific version number of the component document.
3. Use a specific version label of the component document.
4. Do not fix a specific version and allow the component version to be determined at snapshot time. This option is typically useful for applications that can take user input or preferences into account to make this decision.

At the virtual document level, a **standard binding rule** (default version level) can be specified for its components. The setting uses CURRENT by default, and applies to all components that don't have a more specific binding rule specified (are not fixed to a specific version).

The standard binding rule is visible with the label Default Child Version in the Virtual Document Manager figure shown earlier in this chapter.

A virtual document is an evolving document. For example, consider a book being managed as a virtual document for which no specific binding rules have been set. This means that the virtual document always considers the current versions of descendants to be participating the hierarchy. If a chapter document is versioned, the new current version of the chapter becomes a part of the book. The complete state of a virtual document at a point in time can be recorded or archived using a **snapshot**.

A snapshot of a virtual document describes how to archive an *edition* of a virtual document at a particular point in time. It records the exact structure of the virtual document at that point in time and enables its retrieval later when the virtual document may have changed. In one sense, it is a *version* of the complete virtual document hierarchy.

A snapshot of a virtual document is stored using objects of type dm_assembly, where each assembly object represents a component in the virtual document hierarchy. The next figure illustrates how dm_assembly objects represent a snapshot of a virtual document. The hierarchy in the middle shows a virtual document named book. (Versions of each component are shown as stacked boxes.)

Suppose a snapshot of a book named book_snap was created. Later on Chapter1 and Section1.1 were versioned. The snapshot is represented by a dm_document object named book_snap and each of the components is represented by a dm_assembly object in the snapshot. All of the dm_assembly objects in this snapshot point to book_snap via their book_id property. The dm_assembly object corresponding to Chapter2 illustrates some key attributes.

The represented component is pointed to via component_id. The chronicle ID of the component is stored in component_chron_id. The parent of the represented component is stored in parent_id. The level in the virtual document is represented by depth_no, where the depth of the root document is 0. The path up to the component, starting from the root document, is stored in path_name. There is also an order_no attribute, which represents the order among all the components in this hierarchy.

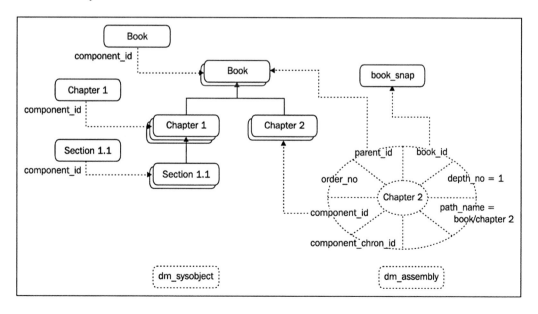

Note that even after a snapshot is taken it is possible for the snapshot to be modified. For example, consider the state illustrated by the previous figure. Now Chapter2 is modified and checked in as the same version. In this case, the virtual document contents retrieved using the snapshot will be different from the contents at the time the snapshot was taken.

It is also possible for Chapter2 to be deleted. In order to prevent such changes to the component versions included in snapshot, the snapshot can be **frozen**. Freezing a snapshot sets r_immutable_flag to 1 on component versions included in the snapshot and prevents deletion or alteration of the content of these versions. A frozen snapshot can later be **unfrozen** as well to allow modifications.

A snapshot can also be viewed just like a virtual document using the Virtual Document Manager component.

Help—Some DQL Queries

DQL provides the keyword IN for checking direct membership of a component in a virtual document. Suppose that the virtual document in the book example has the object ID 0900006480002533. The following query retrieves information about all the chapters and the virtual document itself:

```
SELECT r_object_id, object_name
FROM dm_sysobject
IN DOCUMENT ID('0900006480002533')
WITH ANY r_version_label = 'CURRENT'
```

If all the descendants in the hierarchy are desired, the keyword DESCEND can be used after ID().

Further, suppose that books are being represented as a custom type book_doc and stored somewhere in the folder tree under a cabinet named books. The following query retrieves the names of all such books:

```
SELECT object_name
FROM book_doc
WHERE r_is_virtual_doc = 1
AND FOLDER('/books', DESCEND)
```

Documentum Product Notes

Webtop supports virtual document preferences for users, as shown:

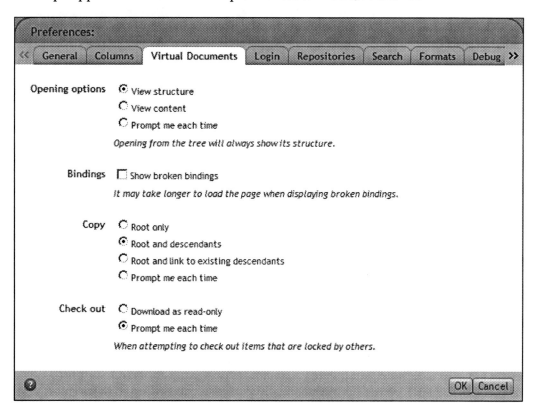

These preferences specify the default behavior on opening, copying, or checking out a virtual document. Opening a document can mean opening the structure of the document or opening the content of the root virtual document object, if it does have any content. A user may choose one of these alternatives or to be prompted when opening a virtual document.

Similarly, copying a virtual document may mean any of the following:

- Only the root document is to be copied.
- The root document is to be copied along with the links to the existing components.
- All the descendants are also to be copied.

The user may choose one of these alternatives or to be prompted when copying a virtual document.

If the user attempts to check out an item as a part of the virtual document and it is locked by another user, the only options for the user are to cancel the operation or to obtain a read-only copy. The user may specify a preference to get a read-only copy or to be prompted each time.

The user may also specify a preference to show **broken bindings**, which shows the descendants linked from the virtual document hierarchy that are no longer present in the repository.

XML content is hierarchical by nature and Documentum provides rich XML management capabilities via **XML applications**, which make extensive use of virtual documents. The capabilities of XML applications include:

- Chunking out content and granting different permissions to different groups for accessing content chunks

- Reusing content chunks in multiple documents and publishing them to multiple locations

- Using XML chunks as wrappers for non-XML documents

- Constructing Web pages dynamically with XML content chunks

XML applications can automatically recognize various types of XML documents and rules can be set up for aspects such as storage locations, need to create chunks, extraction and assignment of metadata, security configuration, etc. On import or checkin, the XML content is automatically processed according to these rules, facilitating efficiency and robustness in XML content management.

Checkpoint

At this point you should be able to answer the following key questions:

1. What are virtual documents? What purpose do they serve?

2. How are virtual documents created and managed?

3. How do component versions affect virtual documents? What options are available for managing versions with virtual documents?

Test Your Understanding

1. A virtual document enables multiple users to collaborate for creating one document (True/False).

2. A virtual document is stored as an object of the following type:

    a. `dm_virtual_doc` or its subtype

    b. `dm_vdocument` or its subtype

    c. `dm_sysobject` or its subtype

    d. None of the above

3. A virtual document can have objects of the following types as components:

    a. `dm_document`

    b. `dm_folder`

    c. Virtual document

    d. None of the above

4. At any time, a document can be a component of:

    a. At most one virtual document

    b. Any number of virtual documents

    c. Any number of virtual documents, as long as they don't share any components

    d. None of the above

5. Components in a virtual document follow these constraints:

    a. All components have the CURRENT version

    b. All components have the same version, but it doesn't have to be current

    c. Each component can have any version independently of the other components.

    d. None of the above

6. Once a snapshot of a virtual document has been created, it is always possible to recreate the exact same state of the virtual document (True/False).

7. An object of `dm_assembly` type represents:

    a. One snapshot of a virtual document

    b. One object's membership in virtual documents

    c. One component of one snapshot

    d. None of the above

8. An object of `dmr_containment` type represents:

    a. One component of a snapshot

    b. One parent-child relationship in one virtual document

    c. One virtual document

    d. None of the above

9. An object cannot be deleted while it is a component of a virtual document (True/False).

10. The Content Server honors the virtual document preferences for a user (True/False).

Practice Test 1

Practice tests are immensely valuable for test preparation since they provide a reality check on the candidate's readiness and point to the areas that need additional work. They are also useful in gauging if any tuning is necessary with regard to meeting the time limit for the test.

 Always read the instructions carefully before starting the test. You will find the real test to be somewhat different and, therefore, it is even more important to pay attention to the instructions. Initially, do not spend more than a few seconds on a question that you are not sure about. Mark it and move on so that you are able to answer all the questions that you know the answers to. Afterwards, revisit the marked questions and answer them. There is no negative scoring so make sure you answer all the questions, even if you have to guess the answers.

Instructions

Select all correct answers — each question can have multiple correct choices. You have 90 minutes to answer the following 60 questions.

Test

1. Which of the following is (are) not a valid data type(s) for an attribute?
   a. Boolean
   b. Number
   c. Double
   d. Date

2. Which of the following is (are) valid lifecycle operation(s) available in Webtop?

   a. Validate

   b. Install

   c. Apply

   d. Promote

3. The Content Server is responsible for:

   a. Creating a repository

   b. Managing content and metadata in a repository

   c. Creating full-text indexes for content in a repository

   d. Enforcing security for content in the repository

4. Which of the following statements is (are) true about virtual documents?

   a. Any sysobject can be a component of a virtual document.

   b. Checking out the root document automatically locks all the components of a virtual document.

   c. Components of a virtual document can be in different formats.

   d. A new version of a component document always replaces the existing one in the containing virtual document.

5. Using a web browser as a client for a WDK application, which of the following is (are) required for accessing content from a Documentum repository?

   a. Application Server

   b. Content Server

   c. Index Server

   d. Webtop

6. A workflow:

   a. Models a business process

   b. Is a sequence of states that a document passes through

   c. Is a network of activities

   d. Must have all the performers uniquely identified before it can start

7. A lifecycle:

    a. Is a linear sequence of activities

    b. Models business rules

    c. Identifies all types it can be applied to

    d. Can have multiple exception states

8. Which of the following statements is (are) true about ACL and ACL templates?

    a. Both ACL and ACL templates are stored in `dm_acl` objects.

    b. An ACL template can be private.

    c. Both ACL and ACL templates can contain alias references.

    d. Each ACL is an instance of some ACL template.

9. An alias can be a placeholder for:

    a. User

    b. Group

    c. Sysobject

    d. Alias set

10. Extended privileges pertain to:

    a. Creating a type

    b. Changing location

    c. Changing state

    d. None of the above

11. An object was checked out at version 3.3 and is being checked in with a minor increment. The new version can be:

    a. 3.3

    b. 3.4

    c. 3.5

    d. 3.3.1.0

12. Suppose that an object has ID `0900006480001126`. What can be the object type of this object?

    a. `dm_folder`

    b. `dm_document`

    c. `dm_user`

    d. A subtype of `dm_document`

13. Which of the following conditions will find books with both John and Jane as authors?

    a. `WHERE authors = 'Jane' and 'John'`

    b. `WHERE any authors = 'Jane' and any authors = 'John'`

    c. `WHERE any authors = 'Jane' and 'John'`

    d. `WHERE authors = 'Jane' and authors = 'John'`

14. A DQL query needs to be written to count all the documents that were created in the last month and updated this month. Which of the following attributes would need to be tested?

    a. `r_modify_date`

    b. `r_last_modify_date`

    c. `r_creation_date`

    d. `r_creation_time`

15. There is a need to manage numerous documents that will be created and managed by different sets of people. These documents will be combined into a book. Which <u>one</u> of the following ways is the most suited for satisfying this requirement?

    a. Put each document in a folder of its own.

    b. Create a virtual document to represent the book.

    c. Use Digital Asset Manager to manage this work.

    d. Create a DocApp for each document.

16. Which of the following statements is (are) true about a cabinet?

    a. A folder can be linked into a cabinet.

    b. A lifecycle can be linked into a cabinet.

    c. A cabinet can be linked into a cabinet.

    d. A document can be linked into a cabinet.

17. Which DQL condition finds objects that have good in the subject attribute?

    a. WHERE subject has 'good'

    b. WHERE subject contains 'good'

    c. WHERE subject like 'good'

    d. WHERE subject like '%good%'

18. A connection broker becomes aware of the status of a Content Server in the following manner:

    a. The Connection broker polls the registered Content Server instances periodically.

    b. The Connection broker polls the registered Content Server instances when a client request is received.

    c. The Content Server informs the connection broker when it starts up.

    d. No status is kept, all registered Content Server instances are reported by the connection broker.

19. A document named 2007Taxes.pdf has the following metadata: subject = 'federal', title = '2007 Taxes', and keywords[0] = 'finance'. The report document itself contains the word 'US'. The Index Server is not installed. Which of the following statements is (are) true?

    a. A simple search for 'finance' can find 2007Taxes.pdf.

    b. A simple search for '2007' can find 2007Taxes.pdf.

    c. A simple search for 'Federal' can find 2007Taxes.pdf.

    d. A simple search for 'US' can find 2007Taxes.pdf.

20. A Documentum deployment has full-text indexing enabled. A document was modified and new text was added to it, which included the word '2008'. This word was not present in the CURRENT version, in either content or metadata. A search for '2008' will find this document when:

    a. The modified document has been saved.

    b. The saved document has been checked in.

    c. The checked-in document has been re-indexed.

    d. A specified amount of time has passed after checkin.

21. There is a dynamic group named `on_duty`, which has 10 predefined members but they are considered as non-members at run time, by default. At run time some of these members can be added to `on_duty` by:

    a. Content Server

    b. Webtop

    c. Application Builder

    d. Custom client code

22. Which of the following DQL conditions can return more than one result when querying a repository?

    a. `WHERE object_name = 'mydoc.txt'`

    b. `WHERE i_chronicle_id = '0900006480001126'`

    c. `WHERE r_object_id = '0900006480001126'`

    d. `WHERE ANY keywords = 'good'`

23. A new user has been created in the repository and the user source has not been set explicitly. When this user tries to log in, the Content Server will try to authenticate the user against:

    a. Operating System

    b. The internally stored password

    c. An LDAP server configured in an LDAP config

    d. An installed authentication plug-in

24. An organization has some reference data that its workers have stored in tables. They want these tables to be accessible through DQL. They can use the following type of query for this purpose:

    a. `AVAIL TABLE`

    b. `EXPOSE TABLE`

    c. `CREATE TABLE`

    d. `REGISTER TABLE`

25. A user failed to promote an object in its lifecycle. Which of the following permissions should be granted to this user to resolve this problem?

    a. Write

    b. Version

    c. Change State

    d. Run Procedure

26. A user is trying to copy a file `/Records/Taxes/2007Taxes.pdf` to a folder `/Home/John` but is unable to do so. Which of the following can be a reason for this problem?

   a. The user does not have Read permission on the object `2007Taxes.pdf`.

   b. The user does not have Change Location permission on the object `2007Taxes.pdf`.

   c. The user does not have Read permission on `/Records/Taxes`.

   d. The user does not have Write permission on `/Home/John`.

27. John is working on 8 documents that are located in various folders. He also frequently accesses documents in a particular folder. He works at three different computers. How can he save time in accessing these documents and this folder in Webtop in the best way?

   a. Create shortcuts and save as bookmarks in the browser.

   b. Subscribe to these documents and folder.

   c. Export the documents and work locally.

   d. Check out the document and folder.

28. Jane considers using SQL rather than DQL for better performance. What is (are) the reason(s) she should not take this approach?

   a. DQL is aware of the object model and makes querying simpler.

   b. Using SQL additionally requires either registering tables or directly accessing the database.

   c. SQL can never provide better performance than DQL.

   d. There are no problems with this approach.

29. An organization uses Documentum for managing documents. It would like to utilize the Documentum infrastructure for managing content for its website as well. Which of the following products should be added to the infrastructure for serving this objective?

   a. Website Manager

   b. Web Content Manager

   c. Web Publisher

   d. Website Creator

30. Business users are not able to instantiate a workflow template that they have been using regularly. What is the likely cause of this problem?

    a.   All the workflows created from this template have been halted.

    b.   The workflow template owner has been deactivated.

    c.   The workflow template has been uninstalled for making changes.

    d.   The maximum limit for simultaneous workflows has been reached.

31. Jane is considering some changes to a custom type `janes_doc` that has `dm_document` as the supertype. Which of the following changes will succeed?

    a.   Increase the length of the `string` attribute `course`

    b.   Reduce the length of the `string` attribute `course`

    c.   Add a `double` attribute `cost`

    d.   Drop the attribute `subject`

32. John created a custom type `test_doc`. Now he is trying to drop this type but is failing to do so. This could be because:

    a.   An object of type `test_doc` exists in the repository.

    b.   A supertype of `test_doc` exists in the repository.

    c.   A subtype of `test_doc` exists in the repository.

    d.   A lifecycle is associated with `test_doc`.

33. Jane has created a new DocApp named `janes_docapp`. She wants to look at how the DocApp is stored. She can find the DocApp and its contents:

    a.   On the filesystem of the computer where she used Documentum Application Builder to create the DocApp

    b.   In the repository where she created the DocApp

    c.   On the application server

    d.   On the Content Server

34. John and Jane are collaborating on a virtual document. They would like to use a workflow to involve some reviewers to improve the quality of this document. Which of the following statements is (are) true?

    a.   They must convert the virtual document to simple document in order to use it with a workflow.

    b.   They can use a workflow directly with their virtual document.

    c.   They must place the virtual document and its components into one folder and use the workflow on this folder.

    d.   They must use Business Process Manager to use a workflow with a virtual document.

35. Jane found that that a document she has been using from the repository has changed but its version is still the same. Which of the following can be a cause for this change?

    a. A new document was imported.

    b. The document was modified and checked in.

    c. A cancel checkout has been performed.

    d. A new branch was created.

36. John checked out version 2.5 of an object. When he checks it back in, the new version can be:

    a. 2.6

    b. 2.7

    c. 5.0

    d. 2.5.2.0

37. The i_chronicle_id property of a rendition identifies:

    a. r_object_id of the root object of the version tree

    b. r_object_id of the primary format object

    c. i_chronicle_id of the primary format object

    d. None of the above

38. A custom type resume has dm_document as its supertype. There is an object named resume.doc of type resume and another named document.doc of type dm_document. Which of the following statements is (are) true?

    a. resume.doc inherits all the property values of document.doc.

    b. document.doc inherits all the property values of resume.doc.

    c. resume.doc inherits all the methods of document.doc.

    d. None of the above.

39. Jane is trying to perform some operations on an object through a program that uses DFC. She is logged in as herself and getting permission errors. She can resolve the problem by:

    a. Logging in as a different user in her program

    b. Using IDQL with her ID

    c. Using IDQL with a different user ID

    d. Changing permissions on the object

40. John was sent a portion of a log file for debugging. He found information about one object interesting. The log contained the object ID but no information about its object type. He can obtain some information about the object type using:

    a. The first two digits of the object ID

    b. The 9th and 10th digits of the object ID

    c. The 3rd to 8th digits of the object ID

    d. None of the above

41. Consider the following query:

    ```
    SELECT r_object_id, title
    FROM dm_sysobject
    WHERE object_name = 'john'
    ```

    Which of the following objects can be selected by this query?

    a. An object of dm_document named 'john'

    b. An object of dm_user named 'john'

    c. An object of dm_folder named 'john'

    d. An object of dm_sysobject named 'john'

42. The file dmcl.ini specifies:

    a. Content Server information

    b. Application Server information

    c. Connection Broker information

    d. Database information

43. Which of the following platform components is (are) required to enforce client capabilities?

    a. Client application

    b. Application Server

    c. Content Server

    d. None of the above

44. John created a group named johns_group. Which of the following statements is (are) true?

    a. Jane can create a role named johns_group in the same repository.

    b. Jane can create a domain named johns_group in the same repository.

    c. Jane can create a private group named johns_group in the same repository.

    d. None of the above.

45. Jane has Extended Delete permission on an object. Knowing only this information what can be inferred about her other permissions on this object?

    a. She has Write permission.

    b. She has Version permission.

    c. She has Change Location permission.

    d. None of the above

46. John has Superuser privileges in a repository. What can be said about his permissions in the repository?

    a. He has at least Read permission on all objects.

    b. He has at least Write permission on all objects.

    c. He can obtain Delete permission on all objects.

    d. No inference can be made about his permissions on all objects.

47. The default ACL mode for the server is set to folder. A user creates an object in folder A and then links it to folder B. The final permission set on the object is the same as:

    a. The permission set of the user

    b. The permission set of the type of the object

    c. The permission set of folder A

    d. The permission set of folder B

48. A custom type named my_document needs to be created. Which of the following is (are) correct statements?

    a. my_document can have two supertypes.

    b. my_document can be a supertype of two other types.

    c. my_document can be a supertype of dm_document.

    d. my_document can be a subtype of dm_document.

49. Jane created a custom type `my_invoice` with an attribute `invoice_type`. She also defined value assistance for `invoice_type`. What can she expect from the Content Server in this regard?

    a. The Content Server will start providing value assistance right away.

    b. The Content Server will start providing value assistance after data dictionary has been published.

    c. The Content Server will not provide value assistance because it is not a part of the data dictionary.

    d. None of the above.

50. John created a NULL type named `johns_doc` and Jane created a NULL type named `janes_doc`. Jane created an object named `'jaDoc.txt'` of type `janes_doc`. Now she wishes to change the type of `'jaDoc.txt'` to `johns_doc`. Which of the following statements is (are) accurate?

    a. She can change the type of the object to `johns_doc` in one step.

    b. She can change the type of the object to `johns_doc` in two steps by first changing its type to `dm_sysobject`.

    c. She can change the type of the object to `johns_doc` in three steps by first changing its type to `dm_document`, then to `dm_sysobject`, and finally to `johns_doc`.

    d. This change of type is not allowed.

51. John created a DocApp using Documentum Application Builder (DAB) and inserted a document from the repository into the DocApp. Much later, he realized that it was a mistake and he deleted the document in DAB. As a result:

    a. The document was also deleted from the repository.

    b. The document was unlinked from its primary folder in the repository.

    c. The document was excluded from a DocApp archive created afterwards.

    d. The document was not deleted from the repository.

52. Jane created a virtual document with several component documents, which she wants to take to another repository as a part of a DocApp that she has already created. She also wants the document renditions to be included in the DocApp. What does she need to do to achieve this objective?

    a. Add the root document and all the components to the DocApp individually.

    b. Add only the root document to the DocApp.

    c. Add the root document, all the components, and all the renditions to the DocApp individually.

    d. Depending on the installation options, any of the above three can suffice.

53. John wants to include a cabinet and all of its contents—complete folder structure and linked objects—in his DocApp archive. He wants all the contents to be included each time the DocApp is archived. What is the best approach he can take?

    a. Add the cabinet to the DocApp.

    b. Add the cabinet and all the folders and objects within the cabinet to the DocApp.

    c. Add the cabinet to the DocApp and set the install option to include both the folder structure and content for this cabinet.

    d. Add the cabinet and all the folders underneath and set the install option to include the linked content.

54. Jane wants to query the workflow templates stored in the repository. The type she needs to use in her query is:

    a. `dm_workflow_template`

    b. `dm_wf_template`

    c. `dm_process_template`

    d. `dm_process`

55. John has a developed a lifecycle and he wants the users to be able to use it even if they don't know its exact name. He can:

    a. Make it the default lifecycle for a cabinet.

    b. Make it the default lifecycle for an object type.

    c. Make it the default lifecycle for a workflow template.

    d. This is not possible.

56. Which of the following is (are) true for the Documentum platform?

    a. An alias can represent a permission set.

    b. A permission set template can use alias references as placeholders.

    c. An alias can only represent a user or a group.

    d. The Content Server does not treat alias references differently, compared to regular values.

57. Jane created an alias set named `janes_alias_set`. It included an alias named `supervisor`. This alias can be referenced as:

    a. `%supervisor`

    b. `$supervisor`

    c. `%janes_alias_set%.supervisor`

    d. `$janes_alias_set.supervisor`

58. John wishes to create several virtual documents and is wondering about the relationship between a virtual document and its components. Which of the following is (are) true in this regard?

    a. A virtual document can contain multiple components.

    b. A simple document can be a component of two virtual documents.

    c. A virtual document can be a component of two virtual documents.

    d. A snapshot can be a component of a virtual document.

59. Jane created a virtual document with several components. These components were independently versioned until a point when Jane felt that she needed to preserve the current state of the complete virtual document so that she could retrieve that state later. She should:

    a. Create a snapshot of the virtual document.

    b. Create a snapshot of the virtual document and freeze the snapshot.

    c. Freeze the virtual document and take a snapshot.

    d. Freeze the virtual document, take a snapshot, unfreeze the virtual document.

60. John started a workflow, which has two automatic activities and three manual activities. The automatic activity A1 has high priority and the automatic activity A2 has low priority. Which of the following statements is (are) true about these activities?

    a. A1 will be executed before A2

    b. A2 will be executed before A1

    c. Priority has no role to play in this case

    d. The correct answer depends on information not present above

Practice Test 2

Practice tests are immensely valuable for test preparation since they provide a reality check on the candidate's readiness and point to the areas that need additional work. They are also useful in gauging if any tuning is necessary with regard to meeting the time limit for the test.

 Always read the instructions carefully before starting the test. You will find the real test to be somewhat different and, therefore, it is even more important to pay attention to the instructions. Initially, do not spend more than a few seconds on a question that you are not sure about. Mark it and move on so that you are able to answer all the questions that you know the answers to. Afterwards, revisit the marked questions and answer them. There is no negative scoring so make sure you answer all the questions, even if you have to guess the answers.

Instructions

Select all correct answers—each question can have multiple correct choices. You have 90 minutes to answer the following 60 questions.

Test

1. An organization has deployed two repositories and they want to synchronize content and metadata between the two repositories. This requirement can be best satisfied by using:

    a. Two content servers

    b. Object replication

    c. Federated repositories

    d. Distributed content storage

2. John does not have Sysadmin privileges. He saved a search as `JohnsSearch` and it shows up in his *My Searches* in Webtop. In order for Jane to see this search in her *My Searches:*

    a. The owner needs to be changed for the stored search object
    b. The stored search object needs to be moved to a different location, and permissions need to be changed
    c. The location of the stored search object needs to be changed
    d. Nothing can be done

3. A customer needs to achieve high availability of the Documentum infrastructure. The best choice for achieving this objective is to create multiple instances of (choose one):

    a. Database and Connection Broker
    b. Content Server and Connection Broker
    c. Application Server and Database
    d. Database

4. Jane is debugging workflows and looking at their states. She can find the workflows in the following states:

    a. Draft
    b. Validated
    c. Halted
    d. Installed

5. Jane is inspecting existing workflows in the repository. Which of the following will serve her purpose the best?

    a. Workflow Manager
    b. Workflow Inspector
    c. Workflow Reporting
    d. Task Manager

6. John is designing a solution to this problem. He wants every user to have a backup user who has write permissions to the documents owned by the users. This problem can be best resolved using

    a. Extended permissions
    b. ACL template
    c. Alias sets
    d. Binding rules

7. Jane has Superuser privileges in a repository. She is a member of Managers group. The Managers group has Version permission on an object resume. doc. Without any other information about permissions on this object, Jane has the following effective permissions on this object:

    a. Read

    b. Version

    c. Write

    d. Change Location

8. John has Relate permission on resume.doc. Based on this information, which of the following operations can he perform?

    a. Navigate to resume.doc using Webtop

    b. View the contents of resume.doc

    c. Check out resume.doc

    d. Check in resume.doc as the same version

9. The current version of resume.doc has 5.2.1.4 as implicit version label. This label indicates that:

    a. This version is a major version

    b. This version is a minor version

    c. This version is on a branch originating from version 5.2

    d. This version is on a branch originating from version 5.2.1

10. Jane and John are collaborating on a book, which is being maintained as a virtual document in a Documentum repository. When they released the first edition of the book, Jane created a snapshot of the book called book_1ed so that they could retrieve the state of this edition later, if needed. Next day, Jane noticed that one of John's chapters has been modified. What possibilities can explain this situation?

    a. The modified chapter is a newer version than what is in the snapshot

    b. The snapshot was not frozen so a component can be modified

    c. Snapshot has nothing to do with component versions

    d. Binding rules on the virtual document allowed this change

11. John wants to learn about virtual documents. He created a virtual document called `test` and is trying to add components to it. Which of the following can be added to `test` as components?

    a. The user object for Jane

    b. A `dm_document` object called `resume.doc`

    c. A folder called `invoices`

    d. A cabinet called `Home`

12. Jane created some custom types as follows. The type `my_doc` has supertype `dm_document` and adds a custom attribute `my_doc_id`. The type `my_invoice` has supertype `my_doc` and adds a custom attribute `my_ref_id`. Which of the following is (are) true about these types?

    a. `my_invoice` has an attribute called `authors`

    b. `my_doc` has an attribute called `my_ref_id`

    c. `my_invoice` has an attribute called `my_doc_id`

    d. `my_invoice` has an attribute called `keywords`

13. John is doing development that involves some customizations. His design includes the following elements. Which of these will give him an error?

    a. A custom attribute named `RefID`

    b. A custom type named `my document`

    c. A group with a 34-character name

    d. A custom attribute named `a_bad_item`

14. Jane was facing problems performing certain tasks with Documentum. She obtained Sysadmin privilege to overcome those challenges. Which of the following tasks will she still be unable to do?

    a. Unlock documents checked out by John

    b. Manipulate workflows and workflow templates

    c. Delete system-level ACL's

    d. Grant Sysadmin privilege to John

15. John is using Webtop and wishes to copy and move some files between repository locations. He can use the following feature to do this:

    a. Containment

    b. Clipboard

    c. Relocator

    d. Migration Assistant

16. Jane created a document `invoice.doc` under `/Invoices/May07`. She owns this document and has Delete permission on `invoice.doc`. She realized that this document needs to be placed under `/Invoices/Apr07`. When she attempted to move the document she was unable to do so. What action may be able to help her overcome this problem?

    a. Obtain Change Location permission on `invoice.doc`

    b. Obtain Extended Delete permission on `invoice.doc`

    c. Obtain Write permission on folder `May07`

    d. Obtain Write permission on folder `Apr07`

17. John's department needs a new process to be automated using Documentum. This automation will be adopted in three months but it must be robust and must put tight controls in place. Which of the following are suitable design choices for this requirement?

    a. Quick flow

    b. Send to Distribution List

    c. Custom workflow template

    d. Custom lifecycle

18. Jane is checking in `resume.doc` using Webtop. On the checkin screen she will be able to:

    a. Keep the lock so that she could continue working on it after creating a new version

    b. Choose a new file to set as the content for the new version

    c. Delete the previous version

    d. Select a different chronicle ID

19. John is wondering about metadata storage within a repository. Where can he find the stored metadata?

    a. Depends upon the file store in use

    b. File system

    c. Content Addressed Storage

    d. Relational database

20. Jane is architecting a Documentum deployment. She has a need to serve a large number of repository connections. Which of the following approaches can she use?

    a. Create two Content Server instances and associate them with one repository

    b. Create one Content Server instance and associate it with two repositories

    c. Create two databases for use with one repository and one Content Server instance

    d. The only way to do this is by adding more memory and CPU power to the hardware

21. The Documentum Collaborative Edition adds the following feature(s):

    a. Email server

    b. Virtual documents

    c. Notes

    d. Chat

22. A type `my_document` has supertype `dm_document`. A document `resume.doc` is of type `my_document`. The `authors` property of `resume.doc` is stored in the following repository table:

    a. `my_document_r`

    b. `dm_document_r`

    c. `dm_sysobject_r`

    d. `persistent_r`

23. John is unable to log into a repository. The administrator checks the repository and finds that the user object for John exists. The following reason(s) can explain the situation:

    a. John is using an incorrect password

    b. The user doesn't exist in the user source

    c. The user object is inactive

    d. The user object is locked

24. The repository owner is a special user who is:

    a. OS account used for installing Documentum software

    b. Database owner for the repository database

    c. A repository user specifically marked as repository owner

    d. Each user with Superuser privilege is a repository owner

25. Which of the following is (are) true about privileges?

    a. Privileges are hierarchical

    b. Some privileges imply other privileges

    c. No privilege imply another privilege

    d. None of the above

26. Jane is worried if her client capability will affect what she can do in the repository. Which of the following enforce client capabilities?

    a. IAPI

    b. Webtop

    c. DA

    d. IDQL

27. John created a dynamic group called `safe_users`. He also added John, Jane, and Mary as members through DA. At run-time when this group's membership needs to be evaluated:

    a. Any user can be added to this group

    b. Only John, Jane, or Mary can be added to this group

    c. Custom code is needed for altering the membership

    d. Membership cannot be changed

28. One of the responsibilities of the Content Server is to secure the content in terms of what each user is able to do. For this purpose, the Content Server gives preference to roles over:

    a. Basic privileges

    b. Extended privileges

    c. Client capability

    d. None of the above

29. Jane is inspecting the attributes of a document named `resume.pdf`. She finds that the `acl_domain` for this document is set to `dmadmin`. This means that:

    a. `resume.pdf` is owned by `dmadmin`

    b. ACL of `resume.pdf` is owned by `dmadmin`

    c. `dmadmin` is the repository owner for the repository containing `resume.pdf`

    d. ACL of `resume.pdf` is public

30. John performed an advanced search with various parameters and saved it as `final_search` once he was happy with the results. One week later if he would run the saved search again:

    a. The results could be different from the original results because more matching objects could have been added since the search was saved

    b. The results would be the same since the results were saved in the saved search

    c. The results would be the same since date range was always saved in the search

    d. The results could be different since some objects may have been deleted

31. Jane uses certain documents frequently and finds it cumbersome to navigate to these documents each time in Webtop. She is considering options to access these documents directly without traversing the full folder path. Which of the following options can help her achieve this objective?

    a. She can subscribe to these documents

    b. She can bookmark these documents using shortcuts

    c. She can link these documents to her default folder

    d. She can write queries that use object IDs of these documents

32. John wants to create a new custom type to store three attributes — `dept_id`, `dept_name`, and `dept_manager`. Which of the following should John choose as the supertype for this custom type?

    a. `dm_sysobject`

    b. `dm_document`

    c. `dm_config`

    d. None of the above

33. Jane wants to use a DocApp and is wondering about certain aspects of using DocApps. Which of the following is (are) true about DocApps?

    a. One DocApp can be deployed to multiple repositories

    b. Multiple DocApps can be deployed to one repository

    c. DocApps are managed using Documentum Administrator

    d. DocApps can be versioned

34. John is designing a workflow template and is considering using a reject flow. Which of the following is (are) true regarding a reject flow?

    a. A reject flow and a forward flow out of the same activity can be selected simultaneously

    b. A reject flow is required from each activity

    c. Multiple reject flows can be defined out of one activity

    d. None of the above

35. Jane wants to use a virtual document to organize hierarchical content. However, she is not sure about certain aspects of the root object in a virtual document. Which of the following statements is (are) correct about the root object in a virtual document?

    a. The root object can have content associated with it

    b. The root object must be a content-less object

    c. The root object must be of type `dm_sysobject` or its subtype

    d. None of the above

36. The permission set templates can be created using:

    a. Webtop

    b. Documentum Administrator

    c. Documentum Application Builder

    d. Web Publisher

37. Jane is trying to promote an object in its lifecycle to the next state. The entry criteria for the next state currently evaluate to false. Which of the following is (are) true about this situation?

    a. Jane will succeed in promoting if she has Superuser privilege

    b. Jane will succeed in promoting if she is the lifecycle owner

    c. Jane will succeed in promoting if she is the object owner

    d. Jane cannot succeed until the entry criteria evaluate to true

38. Jane needs to demote an object in its lifecycle and has the minimum permissions needed to do so. The entry criteria for all the states currently evaluate to false. Which of the following is (are) true about this situation?

    a. Jane will succeed in demoting the object

    b. Jane will not succeed in demoting unless she has Superuser privilege

    c. Jane will not succeed in demoting unless she is the lifecycle owner

    d. Jane will not succeed in demoting until the entry criteria of the relevant state evaluate to true

39. John has created an activity template named *Interview Candidate*. He is now designing a workflow template in which he wants to use this activity template. He wants to create two activities from this template and wishes to place them in parallel. Which of the following is (are) true about this situation?

    a. It will give an error because one candidate cannot be interviewed twice in parallel

    b. It will not give an error but it is not recommended

    c. It is not allowed to put two activities from one activity template to be placed in parallel in one workflow template

    d. John will be able to do so without any problems

40. Jane is planning some customizations and the process for deploying them to various environments during development. One thing she is curious to know is how DocApps will be versioned, if that is possible. Which of the following statements is (are) true in this regard?

    a. DocApps cannot be versioned

    b. DocApp version is stored in the archive and preserved when it is installed into another repository

    c. DocApps are versioned but the version is not stored in the archive

    d. When a DocApp archive is installed into a repository, its version is decided by the Content Server in use

41. John has checked out a document currently at version 5.6. While checking in, he chose to check in as major version. Which of the following can be the version after check in?

    a. 5.6.1.0

    b. 6.6

    c. 6.0

    d. 7.0

42. Jane is designing a workflow template and she does not want to explicitly specify activity performers. She has the following choices in this regard:

    a. The user starting the workflow can specify the performers

    b. Performer of one activity can specify the performer of the next activity

    c. The lifecycle owner can specify the performer

    d. Aliases can dynamically resolve performer of an activity

43. John is learning about attribute names with r_ as a prefix. When he started looking at r_version_label in dm_sysobject he got confused. Which of the following is (are) true about r_version_label?

    a. Users cannot assign a value to r_version_label

    b. Users can assign a value to r_version_label

    c. Content Server assigns values to r_version_label

    d. None of the above

44. Jane is working with a document named resume.doc. She added a pdf rendition for it. If the current rendition is at version 2.3, what can be the next minor version?

    a. 2.4

    b. 2.3.1.0

    c. 3.0

    d. None of the above

45. John created a custom type my_report with the supertype dm_document. He now wishes to drop my_report from the repository. What must he ensure before he can succeed in dropping my_report?

    a. There are no objects of dm_document in the repository

    b. There are no objects of my_report in the repository

    c. There are no subtypes of my_report in the repository

    d. There are no subtypes of dm_document in the repository

46. Jane created a custom type `my_report` with the supertype `dm_document`. She also created a custom type `my_document` with the supertype `dm_document`. She also created an object of type `my_document` named `test.doc`. She wants to change the object type of `test.doc`. Which of the following statements is (are) true in this regard?

    a. It is not possible to change the type of `test.doc`

    b. The type of `test.doc` can be changed to `dm_document` in one step

    c. The type of `test.doc` can be changed to `my_report` in one step

    d. The type of `test.doc` can be changed to `my_report` in two steps

47. John created a custom type with a `string` attribute `report_type` and a `boolean` attribute `is_published`. He wants to define value assistance for these attributes. Which of the following statements is (are) true in this regard?

    a. Value assistance can be defined for `report_type`

    b. Value assistance cannot be defined for `is_published`

    c. Value assistance can be defined for `is_published` only if it has exactly two values

    d. None of the above

48. A subtype inherits the following from its supertype:

    a. Attributes

    b. Methods

    c. Events

    d. None of the above

49. Jane is wondering about the type of a virtual document. A virtual document is stored as an object of the type:

    a. `dm_virtual_document` or its subtype

    b. `dm_vdocument` or its subtype

    c. `dm_sysobject` or its subtype

    d. `dm_document` only

50. When the performer of an activity is specified using an alias reference, for successful resolution the matched alias can be of the type:

    a. User

    b. Group

    c. Permission set

    d. Location

51. Jane has created an alias set named `executives`. One of the aliases in the set is named `ceo`. Which of the following can be used as alias references with a potential match in this alias set?

    a. `%executives.ceo`

    b. `%ceo.executives`

    c. `%ceo`

    d. `%executives.ceo%`

52. John has created a custom type called `my_report` with an attribute named `approver`. He wants to use an alias reference in this attribute to dynamically assign the real approver at an appropriate time. Which of the following statements is (are) true in this regard?

    a. Content Server will recognize an alias reference by the presence of `%` in the attribute value and resolve it

    b. Custom code must be written to resolve such an alias reference

    c. Webtop can resolve such alias references with appropriate configuration

    d. None of the above

53. Jane is designing a lifecycle for the custom type `my_report`. She wants to add exception states to the lifecycle to handle special situations. Which of the following statements can she rely on?

    a. One normal state can be associated only with one exception state

    b. She will be able to demote an object from a normal state to an exception state

    c. One exception state can be associated with only one normal state

    d. An object must always resume from an exception state to the same normal state

54. John is going on vacation and is worried about all the workflows that would need him to participate. The best way to deal with this situation is to:

    a. Let the tasks wait in the Inbox and work on them after he is back from vacation

    b. Get someone to work on his tasks and make himself unavailable

    c. Get himself removed from the performer groups so that no tasks are sent to him

    d. Get the workflows changed so that all activities depending on him are automatically marked complete

55. Jane has received a task in her Inbox. After opening the task she can

    a. Acquire the task

    b. Forward the task

    c. Delegate the task

    d. Ask the task to be Repeated

56. John is using Webtop to perform some operations. He is facing certain security issues which are preventing him from completing his work. In order to troubleshoot the problem, he should consider:

    a. His client capability

    b. His privileges

    c. His extended privileges

    d. His permissions

57. Jane is trying to install a new DocApp archive into a repository but is unable to. The reason could be that

    a. She does not have Superuser privilege

    b. She does not have Sysadmin privilege

    c. She does not have Create DocApp extended permission

    d. She does not have Create DocApp extended privilege

58. Consider the following query and specify which documents it will select:

    ```
    SELECT r_object_id, object_name
    FROM dm_document
    WHERE object_name LIKE '%pdf'
    ```

    a. Documents with an alias reference in `object_name`

    b. Documents with names starting with `pdf`

    c. Documents with names ending with `pdf`

    d. Documents with containing `pdf` anywhere within the name

59. Which of the following statements is (are) true about roles?

    a. A role can be added to a user

    b. A user can be added to a role

    c. A role can be added to another role

    d. A role can be added to a domain

60. An implicit version label:

    a.   Is not visible to end users

    b.   Is assigned by Content Server

    c.   Is assigned by the end users

    d.   Is not used on branches in a version tree

Answers

Chapter 1

1. [False] Any file can be considered to be content. Even though a CSV file contains structured data, it can be stored as content in a repository just like any other file.

2. [c] Metadata is stored in a database.

3. [False] The repository represents the storage unit while Content Server serves content and metadata stored in the repository.

4. [b, c] One Content Server instance is dedicated to one repository but more than one Content Server instance can be dedicated to the same repository.

5. [True] DQL can be used to query any database tables registered to be queried via DQL.

6. [a, d] Calendars and chat are not offered by the collaborative edition of the Content Server.

7. [a, c] Workflows can be defined for documents, folders, and virtual documents.

8. [b, c] Accountability features is provided via auditing and tracing.

9. [b, d] IDQL and IAPI are the interactive query utilities for Documentum.

10. [a, b] ACL and permission set is one and the same thing.

Chapter 2

1. [b, d] 1.0, CURRENT
2. [b, c] Export, Checkout
3. [True]
4. [False] A checkout can also be canceled by a superuser.
5. [False] The user can choose to keep the current version on checkin.
6. [a, b, c, d] Any version can be the CURRENT version.
7. [d] A folder cannot be versioned.
8. [a, b, c, d] Checking in with minor version increment can result in 3.5 and major version increment can result in 4.0. However, if 4.0 already exist in the version tree the major increment results in 5.0. If a new branch is being created and one already exists the new version will be 3.4.2.0.
9. [b]
10. [d] `i_chronicle_id` is not a property of a rendition.

Chapter 3

1. [False] inheritance applies to types and not to objects.
2. [True] `dm_folder` does not define any single-valued property of its own.
3. [False] Security is enforced by the Content Server and this behavior is not dependent upon the mechanism of access (DFC or DQL).
4. [09] The object type tag for `dm_document` and its subtypes is 09.
5. [b] These properties are normally managed by Content Server for its internal purposes and not seen by the users or applications.
6. [c] 4. Since records are shared by different properties, the total number of records is the maximum number of values present for any repeating property.
7. [False] `authors` is a property inherited from `dm_sysobject`. `dm_document` does not have any properties of its own and thus no persistence tables of its own.
8. [d] The first two hex digits in `r_object_id` represent a tag for the object type.
9. [True] DQL can be used to query database tables directly, though the tables being queried need to be registered first.
10. [True] A DQL query on a type queries its subtypes as well and `dm_document` is a subtype of `dm_sysobject`.

Chapter 4

1. [False] Some Documentum layers span multiple tiers.
2. [a, c, d] The layers are Application Layer, Component and Development Layer (Interface Layer), Content Services Layer, and Repository Layer.
3. [c] The Index Server creates full-text indexes based on the contents of documents and these indexes are used for searching.
4. [False] The BOF is supported by DFC and it is at a higher level than DMCL.
5. [b] DFC is made available to the .NET platform using a Primary Interop Assembly.
6. [a] A Content Server projects to connection brokers by announcing its status when it starts up.
7. [c] The Connection broker information is stored in `dmcl.ini` on the client machine.
8. [c] DMCL uses RPC capabilities to perform network communication.
9. [b] The WDK components are the Content Server clients in WDK applications.
10. [d] The WDK customization layer is called `custom`, by default.

Chapter 5

1. [False] Authentication establishes the identity of a user while authorization gives the user access to certain functionality or resources.
2. [False] `dm_check_password` is only used on UNIX.
3. [d] A user can be created in the repository without the existence of the corresponding external account. The external account is needed for authentication to succeed in these cases.
4. [False] The database owner for the repository database is called the repository owner.
5. [False] Client applications may choose to enforce client capabilities. Webtop and Desktop clients do enforce them.
6. [False] Document creation is not controlled by privileges.
7. [False] Create Cabinet and Create Type are separate privileges and each of these needs to be explicitly granted.
8. [True] The Superuser privilege includes all Sysadmin privileges.
9. [False] System Administrator client capability would be needed only if the client application is being used to create the user-enforced client capabilities.
10. [True]

Chapter 6

1. [a, c] Roles and domains are also groups, just used in special ways.
2. [False] Only the configured members of the dynamic group can be added as members for the session.
3. [False] The Content Server neither enforces client capability nor any special treatment for roles.
4. [False] The membership of a sub-role implies membership of the super-role.
5. [False] The Content Server does not enforce the private/public nature of roles, clients do.
6. [False] The automatic public and private assignments based on privileges are defaults. The public/private nature can be changed afterwards.
7. [c]
8. [False] `group_admin` and `owner_name` are two separate properties and can have different values.
9. [False] Each group must be named uniquely within a repository.
10. [True]

Chapter 7

1. [False] Extended permissions are unrelated to basic permissions.
2. [False] A permission set and ACL are one and the same.
3. [b, c] The basic permissions are hierarchical and a given permission implies all lower permissions.
4. [False] All except Extended Delete.
5. [False] Custom permission sets are automatically created by the Content Server when permissions for an object are modified.
6. [c] The ACL is inherited only at the time of new object creation. At least one Documentum document indicates that the ACL should be inherited from the new primary folder, if the primary folder is changed. However, it doesn't in version 5.3.
7. [b] There is no change in the primary folder. Further, see the explanation in the answer to question 6.
8. [a, b]
9. [a, b, c, d] As an owner, Jane gets all extended permissions other than Extended Delete, and as a member of world she gets Extended Delete.
10. [b]

Chapter 8

1. [b, c] Jane won't see `JohnsDocuments` folder but can get to the document through search since BROWSE permission lets her see the properties and the object.

2. [b] Without full-text indexing, the keywords property is not used in a simple search, the search is case sensitive, and content is not searched. The name of the document is present in the `object_name` property which is searched.

3. [a, b, c, d] Since full-text indexing is enabled, all searchable properties and content are searched and the matches are case-insensitive.

4. [b]

5. [c]

6. [False] The search stores the criteria only and not the results. The results will depend on the actual objects and their metadata and content.

7. [False] The saved searches are not compatible across applications.

8. [False] Subscription only makes a document available under the Subscriptions node.

9. [False] The shortcut takes the user back into Webtop.

10. [False] Assuming the user is able to get into Webtop, the user still needs appropriate permissions to access the linked object.

Chapter 9

1. [b, d] Each custom type can have 0 or 1 supertype. Custom types cannot be supertypes of the built-in types.

2. [a, c] `dm_document` is a built-in object type and cannot be modified.

3. [d]

4. [c]

5. [b] Since the `my_invoice` only has single-valued properties of its own, it will only use one table `my_invoice_s`.

6. [False] Even though types cannot be versioned, the changes still need to be committed via checkin.

7. [False] The Content Server does not enforce constraints. In fact, it doesn't use data dictionary for its own functionality.

8. [False] The length of a property is used only if the property is of type String.

9. [True] Multiple conditional lists and one default list can be specified for one property.

10. [a, c] The object type can only be changed to the immediate supertype or a subtype of the current type.

Chapter 10

1. [c]
2. [False] DocApp version is not stored in the archive. The new version depends on the existing version in the new repository.
3. [a, c]
4. [b] DocApp can be archived to the file system but the DocApp only resides in the repository.
5. [a]
6. [b]
7. [b]
8. [c]
9. [d]
10. [False] It can have different users and groups with same permissions and privileges.

Chapter 11

1. [False] A workflow template defines a process while a workflow is an instance of the process in execution.
2. [c]
3. [c]
4. [False] They can be selected simultaneously. It is the responsibility of the developer to configure the activity appropriately to prevent this from happening.
5. [True] Aliases help templates to be more portable across repositories and in various business contexts.
6. [a, b, c]
7. [a, b, c] Start Workflow, Start Attachments, Quick Flow
8. [a, b]
9. [False]
10. [True] A user is marked unavailable by specifying a proxy.

Chapter 12

1. [False] While workflows and lifecycles provide rich capabilities together, they can be used independently of each other.
2. [b, c] A lifecycle must be installed in a repository for use and it is used by applying to objects.
3. [False] Demoting to a state does not check for entry criteria.
4. [a, b] Either all actions in a lifecycle are implemented in Java or all are implemented in Docbasic.
5. [False] A user can apply the default lifecycle for an object type without knowing the name of that lifecycle.
6. [True] In addition to entry criteria being met, the entry actions must also complete successfully.
7. [c]
8. [a]
9. [a]
10. [a, b, c, d]

Chapter 13

1. [False] An alias set contains name-value pairs while a permission set grants permissions to different accessors.
2. [True] Alias references are only present in permission set templates, not in the other types of permission sets.
3. [a, b, d]
4. [c, d] The type name and property name are mismatched in a and b.
5. [True] This is what aliases are for and the `folderSpec` argument can contain an alias reference.
6. [c, d]
7. [c] One custom permission set is created per object, as the permission set template is assigned to objects.
8. [a, b] Only the alias set attached to the object is examined. If no alias set is attached then no alias sets are examined.
9. [a, b, c]
10. [c]

Chapter 14

1. [True]

2. [c]

3. [a, c]

4. [b]

5. [c]

6. [False] If the snapshot is not frozen the component documents can be deleted or checked in as existing versions. Both of these actions can alter the overall contents of the virtual document.

7. [c]

8. [b]

9. [False] A missing object from the virtual document hierarchy results in a broken binding.

10. [False] Virtual document preferences are used by applications such as Webtop.

Practice Test 1

1. [b, d] Dates are stored as data type `time`.

2. [c, d]

3. [b, d]

4. [c] A folder cannot be a component of a virtual document. Versions of components are dependent on their binding rules.

5. [a, b] The Index server is used for full-text indexing and is not even required to be present in a deployment. Webtop is one WDK application and other WDK applications can be used independently.

6. [a, c] A sequence of states is present in a lifecycle, not a workflow. Performers can be dynamically determined using aliases.

7. [b, c, d] A lifecycle contains states, not activities.

8. [a] Whether an ACL is an ACL template is identified by the `acl_class` attribute (1 = template). If an ACL is private (regular) then it cannot be a template, since this is also determined via `acl_class` (0 = regular). Only ACL templates contain alias references. ACL's can exist without any relation to ACL templates.

9. [a, b] An alias can be a placeholder for user, group, location, or permission set (ACL).

10. [d] Extended privileges pertain to auditing.

11. [b, d] 3.4 normally or 3.3.1.0 if a branch is created.

12. [b, d] The type tag 09 represents `dm_document` and its subtypes.

13. [b] A value in a repeating attribute is tested using the `ANY` keyword.

14. [a, c]

15. [b] Virtual documents are ideally suited to manage hierarchical content such as that of a book.

16. [a, b, d] A cabinet is a top-level folder and cannot be linked into anything.

17. [d]

18. [c]

19. [b] Without full-text indexing, the `keywords` property is not used in a simple search, the search is case-sensitive, and content is not searched. The name of the document is present in the `object_name` property that is searched.

20. [c] The new text needs to be re-indexed before it can be found. A fixed-time delay cannot guarantee re-indexing.

21. [d] A dynamic group membership at run time is altered using custom client code.

22. [a, b, d] `r_object_id` is unique within a repository. All versions of an object have same `i_chronicle_id`.

23. [a] By default, a user is authenticated against the Operating System.

24. [d] `REGISTER TABLE` registers a table to become accessible through DQL queries.

25. [a, c] Write and Change State are the minimum permissions needed to promote.

26. [a, d] Read permission is required for copying. Change Location is needed for moving from the primary folder. If folder security is enabled, Browse is needed on the source folder and Write on the destination folder for copying a file.

27. [b] Subscribing to documents and locations makes them accessible under the Subscriptions node. This information is saved in the repository and is available from all clients (browsers on multiple computers).

28. [a, b]

29. [c]

30. [c] A workflow template cannot be instantiated unless it is in the installed state. Stopped workflows and the active state of the workflow template owner don't affect the availability of the template for creating new workflows. There is no set limit on the number of simultaneous workflows.

31. [a, c] Attribute length cannot be reduced. Only non-inherited attributes can be dropped.

32. [a, c] A custom type can be dropped only if no objects and no subtypes of that type exist in the repository.

33. [b] A DocApp is stored as an object of type dm_application in the repository. A DocApp can be archived to the file system as a DocApp archive.

34. [b] A workflow can use a simple documents, virtual documents, and folders.

35. [b] A document can be checked in as the same version. A new document gets version 1.0. Canceling a checkout does not alter the content of the existing version. A new branch changes the version.

36. [a, c, d] The actual version depends on the existing version tree and whether a minor or major increment is chosen on checkin. A minor increment can result in 2.6. A second branch can lead to 2.5.2.0. A major increment can lead to 5.0. The following figures illustrate the scenario:

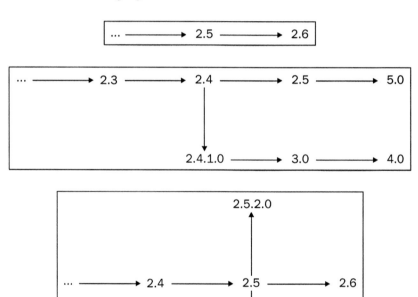

37. [d] `i_chronicle_id` is not a property of a rendition.

38. [d] The inheritance relationship exists between types, not objects.

39. [a, c, d] The Content Server always honors the configured security. If she does not have appropriate permissions on an object she either needs to use a user ID that does have permissions or alter permissions to grant her appropriate access rights.

40. [a] The first two digits of object ID represent the object type or its supertype, which is one of the built-in types.

41. [a, c, d] This query will consider `dm_sysobject` and its subtypes. `dm_user` is not a subtype of `dm_sysobject`. It doesn't even have an attribute named `object_name`.

42. [c]

43. [d] The Client capabilities are optionally enforced by client applications. There is no requirement for client capabilities to be enforced.

44. [d] Roles and domains are also groups. A group must be named uniquely within a repository.

45. [d] Extended Delete is an extended permission and does not imply any other permission, basic or extended.

46. [a, c] A Superuser is a special user and has at least the same effective permissions as the object owner on each object. Each object owner effectively has at least Read permission and all extended permissions other than Extended Delete. The word "effectively" here means that the Content Server will use these effective permissions if the explicitly granted permissions are more restrictive than these. The Change Permission extended permission allows John to grant himself Delete permission explicitly.

47. [c] The object inherits the permission set of folder A since the default ACL mode is folder. Linking the object to folder B does not change its primary folder. Further, the permission set is only inherited when the new object is created.

48. [b, d] Each custom type can have 0 or 1 supertype. Custom types cannot be supertypes of the built-in types.

49. [d] Value assistance is a part of the data dictionary but Content Server does not use the data dictionary for its functionality.

50. [d] The type of an object can only be changed to the supertype or a subtype of the current type. Since both of these types have NULL supertype, it is not possible to change the object type from `janes_doc` to `johns_doc`, even with multiple type changes.

51. [c, d] Removing a document from the DocApp does not remove it from the repository. Also a document no longer in the DocApp is not included in an archive, unless another folder/cabinet includes it and the installation options require the objects to be included as well.

52. [a] The root document and all the components need to be added explicitly. However, renditions are automatically added when a document is added to the DocApp.

53. [c] The best way is to add the cabinet and include the folder structure and objects via the install option. This way, there is minimum onus on the developer and the full folder structure and linked objects are included when an archive is created.

54. [d]

55. [b] The default lifecycle for an object type can be applied to its objects without knowing the name of the lifecycle.

56. [a, b] An alias can also represent a location or a permission set. The Content Server recognizes and resolves alias references in certain attributes and a method argument.

57. [a] Valid references are `%supervisor` and `%janes_alias_set.supervisor`.

58. [a, b, c] A snapshot is stored as an object of type `dm_assembly`, which is not a sysobject. Only sysobjects other than cabinets and folders (and their subtypes) can be components in virtual documents.

59. [b] Only taking a snapshot is insufficient since the component objects and the root object can be altered even in the current version. Snapshots can be frozen, not virtual documents.

60. [d] The answer depends on other factors. If A1 and A2 are sequential within the workflow then the order of execution is determined by the sequence. Priority is used by the workflow agent when multiple tasks corresponding to automatic activities (potentially from different workflows) are ready to be executed at the same time.

Practice Test 2

1. [b]
2. [b] The saved search is stored in Saved Searches in the user's default folder. Appropriate permissions are always needed to access objects.
3. [b] Two content servers can serve the same repository. Each Content Server can project to two Connection Brokers. Both of these components are essential for a client to connect to and use a repository. Application Server and Database can also use their high-availability features such as clustering, but they are not specific to Documentum infrastructure and not sufficient to make a Documentum repository highly available.
4. [c] Draft, Validated, and Installed are states of the workflow template not of the workflow.
5. [c] Workflow Manager is used for designing workflow templates. There is no product/feature in Documentum called Workflow Inspector. Task Manager is used for viewing one particular task.
6. [b, c] Write permission doesn't involve extended permissions. Binding rules relate to virtual documents. An ACL template is one that uses alias references. Aliases are resolved using alias sets. An ACL template can refer to an alias named backup. This reference can be resolved for each case using the owner's alias set.
7. [a, b, d] A Superuser automatically gets the owner permissions on all objects in the repository. The object owner always has Read and all extended permissions other than Extended Delete on the object. This gives Jane Read and Change Location. She gets Version permission via membership of Managers. With the given information, a Write permission cannot be inferred.
8. [a, b] Relate implies Browse and Read permissions. These permissions do not allow checking out or modifying the contents.
9. [b, c] The major version is always of the form x.0. Implicit version labels always have an even number of components separated by dots. 5.2.1 is not a valid implicit version label.
10. [a, b] Binding rules indicate which component versions are part of the virtual document, they do not prevent changes to components. Freezing a snapshot does affect what can be done to a component that is a part of the snapshot.
11. [b] Only sysobjects and their subtypes excluding folders and their subtypes can be virtual document components. Further, dm_cabinet is a subtype of dm_folder.

12. [a, c, d] The attributes are inherited by subtypes from supertypes, so my_doc cannot inherit my_ref_id from my_invoice.

13. [a, b, c, d] Attribute names must use lower-case letters and cannot start with a_. A type name cannot contain a space. A group name can have up to 32 characters.

14. [a, c, d] These tasks require Superuser privilege.

15. [b]

16. [c, d] As an owner she already has Change Location permission. Extended Delete does not give her anything more than the Delete permission that she already has. So the problem is likely due to folder security. Since she is attempting to move, both unlinking and linking are involved. Thus, she needs Write permission on both the source and the destination folders.

17. [c] Quick Flow and Send to Distribution List are the same and provide a simple ad hoc workflow mechanism. Since there is sufficient time to design and test the workflow and the needs are custom, a custom workflow template is ideally suited. A lifecycle doesn't model a process—it rather models various stages for a document and transitions among them.

18. [a, b] Checkin affects the current or next version. A chronicle ID cannot be changed—that would mean moving from one version tree to another.

19. [d] The other options relate to content storage.

20. [a] The question is about one repository. Repository connections are handled by Content Server. Better hardware is not the only solution for this problem.

21. [c] From this list, notes are the only feature added by the collaborative edition. Other supported collaborative features are rooms, discussions, and contextual folders. Virtual documents are supported by the Content Server.

22. [c] dm_document has no attributes of its own and authors is a repeating property of dm_sysobject.

23. [a, b, c, d]

24. [b]

25. [b] Superuser privilege implies Sysadmin privilege. Sysadmin privilege implies all privileges other than Superuser privilege.

26. [b, c]

27. [b, c] A dynamic group can be used as Members-by-default or Non-members-by-default. The membership can be changed only among the pre-defined members using custom code at run time.

28. [d] Content Server does not attach any meaning to roles. Roles and client capabilities are used by applications.

29. [b] The ACL domain of an object is the owner of the ACL of that object. Even though `dmadmin` is the commonly used name for the repository owner, the name `dmadmin` doesn't imply that it is repository owner. An ACL owned by the repository owner (`dm_dbo`) is available to all users.

30. [a, d] Saving a search saves the search criteria. Running the saved search performs the search again and the result depends on the matching objects present at the time of performing the search.

31. [a, b, c, d] All of these are valid options. Subscribing to a document shows it under the Subscriptions node. A shortcut accesses a particular object, with a possible need for authentication. Objects linked to the default folder show up under Home Cabinet. An object ID uniquely identifies an object within a repository.

32. [d] These attributes are going to represent departments. Further, there is no information to indicate the need of any other attributes. So it should not use any type as a supertype and should be created as a NULL type.

33. [a, b, d] DocApps are managed using Documentum Application Builder.

34. [a]

35. [a]

36. [c] As of version 5.3, permission set templates cannot be created using Documentum Administrator.

37. [a, b] Lifecycle criteria are not enforced for the lifecycle owner and for users with Superuser privilege.

38. [a] Entry criteria are not evaluated when demoting an object in its lifecycle.

39. [c]

40. [c, d]

41. [c,d] The major versions are of the form x.0. The new version can be 7.0, if 6.0 is already present in the version tree.

42. [a, b, d]

43. [b, c] `r_version_label` is an exception to the rule that attributes with names prefixed with `r_` are read-only for users. The Content Server assigns an implicit version label and the CURRENT version label. Users can assign their own symbolic version labels.

44. [d] Renditions cannot be edited or versioned.

45. [b, c]

46. [b, d] The type of an object can be changed to its supertype or subtype in one step. So the type of test.doc can be changed from my_document to dm_document in one step, and then from dm_document to my_report in another step.

47. [a, b] Value assistance cannot be defined for boolean attributes.

48. [a, b, c]

49. [c] A virtual document can be of the type dm_sysobject or its subtype other than dm_folder and its subtypes.

50. [a, b]

51. [a, c]

52. [b] The Content Server recognizes alias references only in specific predefined attributes and in the argument of the link and unlink DFC methods. See the chapter *Aliases* (Chapter 13) for more details.

53. [a] The transition to an exception state is called suspension. Multiple normal states can use one exception state. The lifecycle resumes to the normal state from which it was suspended.

54. [b] John should mark himself unavailable and identify a proxy to work on his tasks. Once he is back, he can mark himself available again.

55. [a, b, c, d] All of these options are possible though some may depend on the configuration in the workflow template.

56. [a, b, c, d] Webtop honors client capability and Content Server enforces privileges, extended privileges, and permissions.

57. [a] Creating a DocApp requires Superuser privilege. There is no such thing as Create DocApp extended permission or extended privilege.

58. [c] The Content Server doesn't look for alias references in object_name. The keyword LIKE uses the % symbol for pattern matching.

59. [b, c, d]

60. [b] The version numbers are implicit labels and are assigned by the Content Server.

Index

API 20
IAPI 21
IDQL 21
web development kit 21
DocApps
about 143
archiving 146-148
creating 144
DAB 144
DocApp archive 144-146
Document Application Installer 148
installing 148
installing process 149
managing 144
modifying 144
objects 145
prerequisites 149
properties 143
Document Application Installer 148
document query language. *See* DQL
Documentum
aliases 185
application layer 56
architecture 49
authorization 83
business process 153
communication patterns 58
component and development layer 54
content 15
content, hierarchically managing 199, 200
content, working with 23
content server 17
content service layer 52
customizing 141, 142, 185
custom types 125
DocApp 143
Documentum Application Builder 126
domain 88
integration services 57
layered architecture 50
lifecycles 169
metadata 15
objects 33
object security 91
object types 35, 125
platform 49
privileges 69

product notes 31
repository 16, 17
repository layer 51
roles 87
searching 105
security 69
terminology 15
user privileges 69
user roles 87
vitual documents 199
workflows 153
workflow template 154
Documentum Application Builder
about 126
custom types, creating 126
DocApps 144
information needed, for creating custom
type 128
uses 126
domain 88
DQL
about 41
basics, SELECT query 42, 43
DELETE query 45, 46
registered table 41
SELECT query 41-44
UPDATE query 44
WHERE clause, SELECT query 43, 44

E

ECIS 109
EMC Documentum. *See* **Documentum**
enterprise content management
basics 15
Documentum terminology 15
events
about 129
application event 129
system event 129

F

frequently accessed objects
about 117
shortcuts 117
subscriptions 117

About Packt Publishing

Packt, pronounced 'packed', published its first book *"Mastering phpMyAdmin for Effective MySQL Management"* in April 2004 and subsequently continued to specialize in publishing highly focused books on specific technologies and solutions.

Our books and publications share the experiences of your fellow IT professionals in adapting and customizing today's systems, applications, and frameworks. Our solution based books give you the knowledge and power to customize the software and technologies you're using to get the job done. Packt books are more specific and less general than the IT books you have seen in the past. Our unique business model allows us to bring you more focused information, giving you more of what you need to know, and less of what you don't.

Packt is a modern, yet unique publishing company, which focuses on producing quality, cutting-edge books for communities of developers, administrators, and newbies alike. For more information, please visit our website: www.packtpub.com.

Writing for Packt

We welcome all inquiries from people who are interested in authoring. Book proposals should be sent to authors@packtpub.com. If your book idea is still at an early stage and you would like to discuss it first before writing a formal book proposal, contact us; one of our commissioning editors will get in touch with you.

We're not just looking for published authors; if you have strong technical skills but no writing experience, our experienced editors can help you develop a writing career, or simply get some additional reward for your expertise.

Printed in the United States
88759LV00005B/23/A